Aldo Ivanišević

EAT & LOVE CROA

The CROATIAN COOKBOOK

Copyright 2019 by Aldo Ivanišević

ALDO IVANIŠEVIĆ

EAT & LOVE
CROATIA

The CROATIAN COOKBOOK

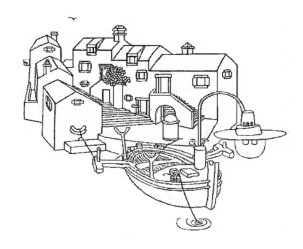

TABLE
OF
CONTENTS

◊

FOREWORD

Top 11 dishes you must eat while visiting Croatia:

Cheese, young or mature, prosciutto and black olives, possibly accompanied by salted anchovies or capers.

Seafood platter - a real delicacy of the adriatic region.

Buzara - scampi or mussels, shortly cooked with white wine, garlic, parsley and breadcrumbs.

Black risotto - colored black because of the cuttlefish ink.

Oysters - served immediately after being removed from the sea, enriched with lemon juice.

Grilled fish - unavoidable dish when in the adriatic region.

Zagreb steak - veal steak stuffed with ham and cheese, breaded and fried

Pashtitsada - beef marinated in vinegar, and after that braised for hours

Lamb, veal or octopus under the bell (Peka) - the slow-cooking process makes the meat tender and the potatoes very tasty.

Strukli - delicious pastry, filled with cottage cheese and sour cream

Rozata - the most popular dessert in the Dubrovnik region

SOUP

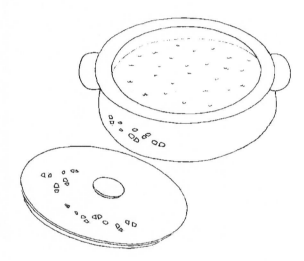

OYSTER SOUP

Ingredients

oysters 15-20
cooking cream 50-100 ml
bread crumbs 1 tbsp
olive oil 3-4 tbsp
garlic 1-2 cloves
salt, pepper
parsley

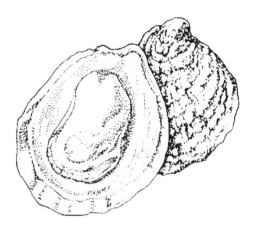

Preparation

Shuck the oysters and remove the meat from the shells. Chop the oyster meat, some finely, some coarsely. Finely chop also the garlic and parsley.

Heat the olive oil in a pot and put in the chopped oyster meat, garlic and half of the chopped parsley. Stir in also the bread crumbs. Fry over low heat for a minute or two, stirring all the time.

Pour into the pot one litre of water Cover the pot and cook for a while, not long.

Then remove the soup from the heat and stir in the cream, salt and pepper, and the remaining parsley.

Optional ingredients

Dry white wine, fish soup or stock, shrimp tail meat, mussel meat, flour, gently fried in oil, butter, lemon juice and/or zest, nutmeg, yolk, tomato paste, fresh tomatoes, minced onion, grated carrot, basil, oregano, chopped celery, boiled rice or soup pasta, finely chopped fennel, milk, paprika, bell pepper, leeks, dried bacon, boiled potatoes, boiled small white beans, vegetable bouillon powder, bay leaves.

MUSSEL SOUP

Ingredients

mussels 1 kg fresh or 500 g frozen
fresh tomatoes, finely chopped, 1-2
or
tomato paste 1-2 tsp
dry white wine 50-100 ml
bread crumbs 1 tbsp
olive oil 3-4 tbsp
garlic 1-2 cloves
salt, pepper
parsley

Preparation

Clean the mussels and tap any mussel that is open. Discard the ones that do not close after being tapped. Then rinse the mussels under tap water.

Heat the mussels in a covered pot

(no water added) until they open themselves. Then remove the meat from the shells and chop it coarsely. Discard the shells that haven't opened up during the heating process.

Leave a few opened shells with the meat still inside.

Finely chopp the peeled garlic cloves and the parsley leaves. Peel the tomatoes and then chop them.

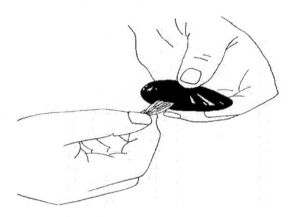

Heat the olive oil in a pot and put in the chopped mussel meat, the garlic and half of the chopped parsley. Stir in also the bread crumbs. Fry over low heat for a minute or two, stirring all the time. Add the tomatoes and pour in the wine. Continue cooking over medium heat, letting the wine almost evaporate.

After that pour into the pot one litre of water. Cover the pot and cook for a while, not long.

Then remove the soup from the heat and stir in the salt and pepper, as well as the remaining parsley.

Optional ingredients

Dry white wine, fish soup or stock, shrimp tail meat, lemon juice and/or zest, tomato paste, fresh tomatoes, minced onions, boiled rice or soup pasta, boiled potatoes, vegetable bouillon powder, bay leaves, celery, peperoncino, white vinegar, carrot, thyme, milk, cooking cream, parmesan cheese, butter, oregano.

TOMATO SOUP

Ingredients

fresh ripe tomatoes 1 kg
olive oil 3-4 tbsp
garlic 1-3cloves
salt, pepper
rice 20-50 g
onion 1
parsley

Preparation

Peel the tomatoes and chop them finely. Chop also the onion, garlic and parsley.

Fry the onions in a pot, over low heat. After a couple minutes add the garlic and parsley. Stir a couple of times and then put the tomatoes. Stir again. At this moment, the tomatoes may be minced with an immersion blender (stick mixer). Then add the rice. Cook until the rice is boiled enough. Season with salt and pepper.

eat and love Croatia

Optional ingredients: Basil, bread crumbs, sugar, bell pepper, potatoes, carrots, leeks, peperoncino, vegetable bouillon powder, celery, dried bacon, sage, rosemary, bay leaves, dry white wine, cooking cream, sour cream, barley, red lentils.

Optional ingredients at the end: Parmesan cheese, basil, parsley, sage, minced pickles.

Optional ingredients: tomato paste, fresh tomatoes, garlic, vegetable or meat bouillon powder, bay leaves, peperoncino, pine nuts, beans, broad beans, corn, peas, lentils, tomato paste, sage, flour, gently fried in oil.

Optional ingredients at the end: parmesan cheese, parsley, cooking cream, yolk, vinegar, lemon juice.

BARLEY SOUP

Ingredients

barley 100 g
dried bacon (pancetta) 100 g
olive oil 3-4 tbsp
salt, pepper
potato 1-2
carrot 1
celery 1
onion 1
leek 1

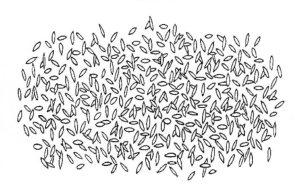

Preparation

Cook the barley in a pot, in a litre of water.

After 1,5 hours or so, add the onions, leek, celery, carrot and potatoes, all chopped or grated. Also put in the bacon, cut into pieces. Keep on cooking until all the vegetables are boiled enough.

CUTTLEFISH SOUP

Ingredients

cuttlefish 500-700 g
olive oil 3-4 tbsp
garlic 1-2 cloves
salt, pepper
onions 1-2
parsley

Preparation

Clean the cuttlefish and cut it into small pieces. Save the cuttlefish ink. Chop the onions, garlic and parsley.

Heat the oil in a pot. Fry the onions over low heat. After a couple of minutes, add the garlic and parsley. Keep cooking for a few minutes more, stirring all the time.

Put in the cuttlefish and let it cook for 20-30 minutes. Then pour in a litre of water. Season with salt and pepper and stir in the cuttlefish ink, previously dissolved in some water. Shortly after that, remove the pot from the stove.

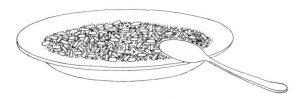

Optional ingredients: rice, leeks, vegetable bouillon powder, fish soup, bay leaves, rosemary, shell meat, scampi or shrimp meat, tomato paste, thyme, dry white wine.

Optional ingredients at the end: lemon juice, vinegar, peperoncino.

Note: In the middle ages, it was beleived that this is a witches' soup, because of its black color.

FISH SOUP

Ingredients

white fish (hake or other) 500 g -1 kg
olive oil 4-5 tablespoons
rice 1-2 tablespoons
garlic 1-4 cloves
salt, pepper

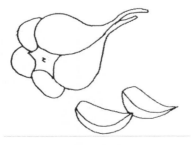

Preparation

Gut and rinse the fish. Finely chop the garlic.

Pour 1.2 liters of water into a pot. Add the fish.

Cover and cook over medium-high heat, until the fish begins to separate from the bones. Then take the fish out of the soup and leave it aside.

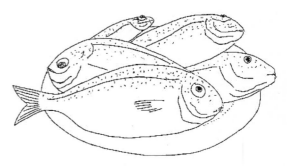

Add the rice into the soup. Continue cooking the soup over medium heat until the rice is cooked "al dente". Then season with salt and pepper, drizzle with olive oil and sprinkle with minced garlic.

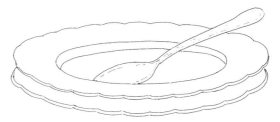

Optional ingredients

Tomato paste or peeled and diced fresh tomatoes, carrots, leeks, onions, celery, scampi or shrimp tail meat, shell meat, zucchini, bell peppers, parsley, bay leaves, vegetable bouillon powder, dry white wine, vinegar, paprika, lemon juice and/or zest.

Note

To obtain a more creamy soup, put a spoonful of rice, or two, at the beginning of cooking the soup. Squash it later, with all other ingredients, well cooked.

In that case omit adding another quantity of rice later on.

CHICKPEA SOUP

Ingredients

dry chickpeas 300 g
olive oil 3-4 tablespoons
(white) onion 1 small
tomato paste 1 tbsp
vegetable bouillon
(powder or cube)
garlic 1-4 cloves
bay leaves 1-2
salt, pepper
rosemary
carrot 1
celery
leek 1

Preparation

Let the chickpeas soak in water until tomorrow. Drain them before further use.

In a pot pour a litre of water and add the drained chickpeas and all the other ingredients.

Cover the pot and cook until the liquid starts boiling. Then continue cooking over low heat, stirring occasionally, for 60 minutes, maybe longer. The chickpeas must be very tender.

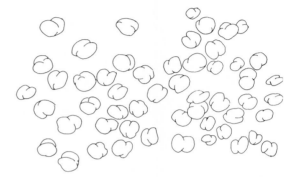

Optional ingredients

Potatoes, leeks, bell pepper, fresh tomatoes, parsley, oregano, thyme, basil, bay leaves, red lentils, soup pasta, rice, barley, zucchini, corn, mushrooms and parmesan cheese, and some olive oil, at the end.

SHRIMP SOUP

Ingredients

shrimp or scampi tails
(fresh or frozen) 600-700 g
bread crumbs 1-2 teaspoons
cooking cream 50-200 ml
dry white wine 50 ml
garlic 1-2 cloves
salt, pepper
lemon 1
parsley

Preparation

Peel the garlic cloves and then crush

them. Finely chop the parsley. Grate the lemon zest using a lemon zester. Then squeeze the juice out of the lemon, being aware that later on just a part of it will be used.

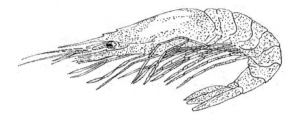

Warm up the oil in a pan and then gently fry the garlic and parsley. Add some bread crumbs and stir a couple of times, still over low heat.

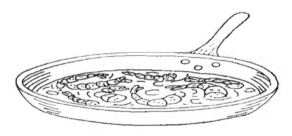

Put in the shrimp tail meat and continue cooking over medium high heat, not for long. Then pour in the dry white wine. Let it evaporate, almost all of it. Add the lemon zest, lemon juice (not much), stir in some cooking cream, as much as you like, but not all at once, stirring all the time while pouring it in. Season with salt and pepper. Pour in enough water and let the soup cook for a couple minutes, over medium high heat.

Before serving the soup, all the ingredients can be minced with a stick mixer (immersion blender).

Optional ingredients: brandy (cognac, armagnac), peperoncino, vegetable bouillon powder, carrot, egg yolk, tomato paste, leek, salted anchovies, pickled gherkins, onions.

LEEK AND COWLIFLOWER SOUP

Ingredients

cowliflower 300-400 g
fresh leeks 2
olive oil 2-3 tbsp
celery 1 branch
garlic 1 clove
salt, pepper
onion 1
parsley

Preparation

Slice the cowliflower and the leeks thinly. Finely chop the onion, garlic, celery and parsley.

Warm up the oil, in a pot, and then gently fry the onions, over low heat. Add the minced garlic, celery and parsley. Stir a few times and then put the prepared vegetables. Cook over medium heat for a couple of minutes, stirring all the time. Then lower the heat and continue cooking the vegetables, stirring occasionally.

When the vegetables are cooked, pour in a litre of water and continue cooking over medium heat for a few minutes more.

eat and love Croatia

CARROT SOUP

Ingredients

carrots 600 g
olive oil 2-3 tablespoons
vegetable bouillon cube 0,5-1
or
powder 1 teaspoon
salt, pepper
onions 1-2

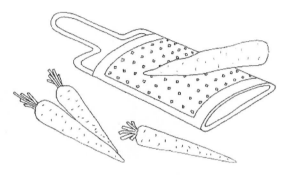

Preparation

Peel the onions and cut them into large pieces. Peel also the carrots and grate them finely.

Warm up the oil, in a pot, and then gently fry the onions, over low heat. Add the carrots and stir a couple of times. Then pour some water and continue cooking, stirring often, over medium heat, until the water almost evaporates.

Pour one litre of water and stir in the vegetable bouillon cube or powder. Cover the pot and continue cooking for another 15-20 minutes.

At the very end, extract the onions and season with salt and pepper.

Optional ingredients

Potatoes, tomatoes, leeks, zucchini, cauliflower, bell peppers, apples, red lentils, peas, celery roots, parsley roots, red paprika, oregano, nutmeg, bay leaves, parsley leaves, bread crumbs, garlic, basil, thyme, saffron, cream, sour cream, milk, honey, lemon zest, marjoram, cloves, and, after taking the pan out of the fire, grated hard cheese or lemon juice.

VEGETABLE SOUP

Ingredients

assorted vegetables 250-500 g
olive oil 2-3 tablespoons
celery 1-2 branches
tomatoes 1-2
garlic 1 clove
salt, pepper
carrot 1
onion 1
parsley

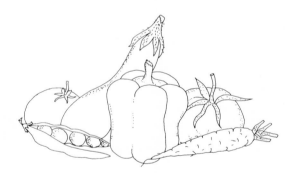

Preparation

Clean, rinse and then cut the vegetables into small bits.

Warm up the oil, in a pot, and then gently fry the onions, over low heat. Add the minced garlic and parsley. Stir a few times and then put the prepared vegetables. Cook over medium heat for a couple of minutes, stirring all the time. Then lower the heat and continue cooking the vegetables, pouring some water and stirring from time to time.

When the vegetables are cooked, pour in a litre of water and continue cooking over medium heat for a few minutes more.

The vegetable soup then can be served or it can be filtered first or even mashed with an immersion blender.

Cooking the soup

For best quality, add the vegetables into the cooking pot gradually, depending on the time needed to cook specific sort. For instance, potatoes need more cooking time then cauliflower.

Ad salt at the end of the cooking process.

Selecting vegetables

The vegetable soup can be prepared using one, two or several vegetable sorts.

The favourite choices are the tomato soup and the carrot soup, but often more sorts are being combined, like potatoes and leeks, for instance.

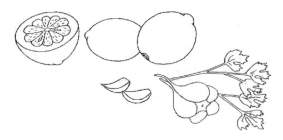

Optional ingredients

Additional seasonings may be used like celery, vegetable bouillon cube or powder, bay leaves, dry white wine, basil, paprika, milk, cooking or sour cream, diced bacon or a piece of a cheese rind.

A special flavor, and also the thickening the soup, can be obtained by adding pasta, rice, red lentils, barley, potatoes, peas, fava beans, bread crumbs, rice or corn flour, or light roux (flour, shortly fried in oil or butter, over a very low heat).

Before serving the soup, its taste can be enriched by adding grated hard cheese, vinegar, lemon juice, chopped parsley, bacon, finely cut to bits, crushed garlic or chopped arugula.

eat and love Croatia

MUSHROOM SOUP

Ingredients

(porcini) mushrooms 250-300 g
(olive) oil or butter 2-3 tbsp
sour cream 1-3 tbsp
dried bacon 50-80 g
onion 1 small
paprika 1 tsp
flour 1 1bsp
salt, pepper
potato 1-2
marjoram
parsley

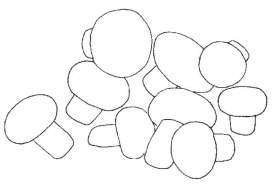

Preparation

Finely slice the mushrooms.Peel the onion and mince it finely. Peel the potatoes and cut them into pieces. Finely chop the parsley and marjoram. Mince the bacon.

Warm up the oil, in a pot, and then gently fry the onions, over low heat. One by one, add the ingredients. Stir all the time. Then pour in some water and continue cooking the soup.

DILL SOUP

Ingredients

fresh dill 100 g
(olive) oil or butter 2-3 tbsp
sour cream 50-100 g
lemon juice 1 tbsp
salt, pepper
flour 1 tbsp
egg yolk 1
onion 1-2

Preparation

Peel the onions and cut them into large pieces. Mince the dill.

Warm up the oil, in a pot, and then gently fry the onions, over low heat. Add the flour and stir a for a minute. Then add and the dill. Stir a few times and then pour in one litre of water. Cover the pot and continue cooking for 15-20 minutes. At the end put in the sour cream, a yolk and some lemon juice, not much.

Optional ingredients: carrots, bread crumbs, garlic, vegetable bouillon cube or powder, egg white, leeks, celery, potatoes, tomato paste.

MANESHTRA

Ingredients

dry beans 200-300 g
or
frozen 500 g
barley 70-100 g
(olive) oil or butter
2-3 tbsp
dried bacon 100-250 g
canned corn 1 can
tomatoes 1-2
or tomato paste
1-2 tbsp
potatoes 2-4
garlic 2-3 cloves
paprika powder
bay leaves 1-3
salt, pepper
carrots 2-3
onion 1-2
parsley

Preparation

Let the beans and barley soak overnight in water.

Cook the beans and barley in in a litre of water, adding all the minced ingredients and spices. A couple of minutes before the soup is cooked, add the corn, paprika and parsley.

Optional ingredients: fennel, wild fennel, dill, dried meat, souerkraut, roux (flour gently fried in olive oil or butter), celery, green beans, lentils.

Optional ingredients at the end: grated cheese.

ZAGORSKA SOUP

Ingredients

mushrooms 200-300 g
vegetable bouillon powder
sour cream 150-200 ml
white wine 50-100 ml
dried bacon 50-100 g
potatoes 300 - 400 g
oil o butter 2-3 tbsp
garlic 1-2 cloves
paprika powder
bay leaves 1-2
flour 1-2 tbsp
salt, pepper
carrot 1
onion 1
parsley
celery

Preparation

Dice or mince all the ingredients.

Warm up the oil, in a pot, and then gently fry the onions, over low heat. One by one, add the ingredients. Stir all the time. Then pour in some water and continue cooking the soup.

Optional ingredients: fresh tomatoes or tomato paste, sugar, thyme.

Note: The Zagorska soup, or Zagorje soup, is a soup which has its origins in the Croatian region of Zagorje.

SLAVONSKA SOUP

Ingredients

dried bacon 100-200 g
oil o butter 2-3 tbsp
garlic 1-2 cloves
paprika powder
flour 1-2 tbsp
sausages 2-4
salt, pepper
leeks 1-2
carrot 1

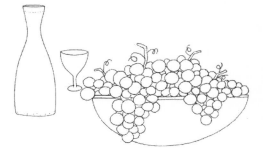

Preparation

Dice or mince all the ingredients. Warm up the oil, in a pot, and then gently fry the onions, over low heat. One by one, add the ingredients. Stir all the time. Then pour in some water and continue cooking the soup.

Optional ingredients: pumpkin seed oil, parsley, celery, onion, potatoes vegetable bouillon powder, broccoli.

Note: The Slavonska soup, or Slavonian soup, Slavonia soup, is a soup which has its origins in the Croatian region of Slavonia.

PASTA

SHPORKI MACARULI
(dirty maccaroni)

Ingredients

pasta (penne, fusilli or other) 400 g
whole peeled (plum) tomatoes,
fresh or tinned 200-400 g
meat (beef or veal) 700 g - 1 kg
tomato paste 1-5 tbsp
red wine 100-200 ml
garlic 1-2 cloves
dry prunes 1-3
salt, pepper
onions 3-5
bay leaves
cinnamon
nutmeg
parsley
cloves

Preparation

Dice the meat. Finely chop the onions. Peel the garlic cloves and mince or crush them. Chop the parsley.

Warm up the oil in a pan and then gently fry the chopped onions, over low heat, until they turn pale gold. At the moment, add the garlic and parsley, bread crumbs, maybe even a tablespoon, or a teaspoon of flour. Stir a couple of times and put in the meat.

Raise the cooking temperature letting the meat braise for a minute or two, stirring all the time. Then pour in the wine. When the wine is almost evaporated, put in the tomato paste or, even better, fresh tomatoes or the ones extracted from the can. Continue cooking, over medium heat, until the liquid evaporates. Then stir in bay leaves, cloves, grated nutmeg, chopped dry prunes, salt and pepper, and a pinch of cinnamon.

Adding a pinch of sugar is optional, as well as the paprika powder, lemon zest, grated nutmeg or a beef bouillon cube or powder.

Continue cooking until the meat is softened enough, what will happen after about two hours, stirring from time to time, pouring in some water or meat soup, if necessary.

Cook the pasta (homemade macaruli i.e. maccaroni, penne or other type of short pasta) in an abundant quantity of salted water. Drain the pasta and season it with the sauce (make it "dirty", in a way).

Grated cheese may be welcomed, before or after serving the pasta.

Potato gnocchi may be used instead of pasta.

Note: This is a traditional dish very popular in the region of Dubrovnik.

PASTA
WITH TOMATO SAUCE

Ingredients

pasta 400 g/14 oz
ripe (plum) tomatoes 0,5-2 kg/1-4 lb
olive oil 5-6 tbsp
salt, pepper
sugar 1 tsp
onions 3-5

Preparation

Peel the tomatoes and cut them into small pieces. After that, warm up the oil in a large saucepan and fry gently the chopped onions, over low heat. Then add the tomatoes. Stir in the salt and sugar. Bring the sauce to a simmer and continue cooking over very low heat.

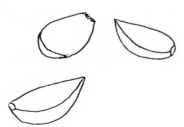

In the meantime, cook the pasta in an abundant quantity of salted water.

Drain the pasta "al dente", mix it with the sauce and serve it promptly.

Basic recipe
for long-lasting cooking
of the tomato sauce

Peel the tomatoes (1.5-2 kg) and cut them into small pieces. Finely chop and mince the onions.

In a large pot, fry the onions in oil, over low heat. When the onions start to change its colour, add the tomatoes.

Cook for 2-3 hours over low heat. At the end add salt and sugar.

Basic recipe
for short-lasting cooking
of the tomato sauce

Peel the tomatoes (1-2 lb, 400-800 g) and cut them into small pieces. Crush the tomato pieces and let the liquid drain off.

Cook the tomatoes over medium heat for 10-15 minutes letting the tomatoes lose its raw taste. Add the sugar and salt.

At the very end of the cooking, possibly blend some crushed or finely chopped herbs into the thickened souce.

Optional basic ingredients, herbs and spices:

Canned plum tomatoes, tomato paste, basil, carrots, bell peppers, parsley, garlic, rosemary, vinegar, aceto balsamico, chili peppers, celery, capers, pine nuts, anchovy fillets, green or black olives, honey, almonds, marjoram, dry white wine, lemon juice or lemon zest, vegetable bouillon powder, nutmeg, cloves, thyme, aubergines, mint, paprika powder, cinnamon, breadcrumbs, mustard, dried tomatoes, cheese, coriander seeds, raisins, sweet wine, oregano, rocket salad, pancetta (dried bacon), (ground) walnuts, roux (flour fried in butter or oil), mushrooms, cream, red wine, canned tuna fish, olive paste, prunes (dried plums), shallots.

Optional ingredients at the end - basil, chives, grated cheese.

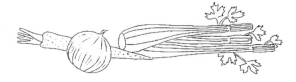

Warning

Do not put too many different ingredients, herbs and spices in the sauce. Add them sparingly, tasting the sauce from time to time, especially when it is already thickened.

PASTA WITH MEAT RAGÙ

Ingredients

pasta 400 g/14 oz
minced (beef or pork) meat 800 g / 2 lb
ripe (plum) tomatoes 500 g / 1 lb
tomato paste 2-3 oz
olive oil 4-5 tbsp
garlic 2-3 cloves
bay leaves 3-7
salt, pepper
onions 1-2
parsley

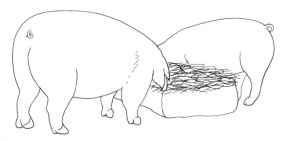

Preparation

Warm up the oil in a pan. Put in the finely chopped onions and let them fry over low heat. Then add the garlic, previously chrushed, as well as the finely chopped parsley. Stir a couple of times, still over low heat.

Then add the meat and increase the heat to medium high.

Cook for 10-15 minutes, stirring often. Add the tomatoes, already cut into small pieces, the tomato paste and the bay leaves.

Cook for half an hour, over medium heat. Stir every now and then. If necessary, pour in some water, not much. At the very end, season with salt and pepper.

Cook the pasta in an abundant quantity of salted water.

Drain the pasta "al dente" (firm to the bite), mix it with the ragù and serve it immediately.

Optional ingredients

Sausages, mushrooms fresh or dry, chicken livers.

Optional herbs and spices

Carrot, celery, red or dry white wine, sugar, pancetta (dried bacon), prosciutto ham, shallots, meat or vegetable soup, nutmeg, cloves, cinnamon, milk, basil, grated lemon zest, green olives, sage, rosemary, prunes, cheese rind, vegetable bouillon powder or cube.

Optional ingredients at the end: grated cheese, cream.

Possible omissions: garlic, parsley.

PASTA
WITH CHEESE SAUCE

Ingredients

pasta 400 g/14 oz
butter or olive oil 5-7 tbsp
grated hard cheese
150-200 g / 5-7 oz
flour 1.5-2.5 oz
milk 2-2.5 cups
nutmeg
salt

Preparation

Melt the butter or oil in a saucepan, over low heat.

Take the pan off the stove and then stir in the flour. Put the pan back to the stove and cook over low heat for 1-2 minutes, mixing constantly.

Move the pan again away from the heat and pour in the milk. Stir for a minute and put the pan back to the stove. Continue cooking for about ten minutes, still over low heat, letting the sauce to thicken gradually. Stir every now and then.

Once again remove the pan from the flame and add the grated cheese, grated nutmeg and later on even some salt (only if really necessary).

Blend the ingredients well, making sure that the sauce does not become too dense. If necessary, thin the sauce with some water.

Cook the pasta in an abundant quantity of salted water.

Drain the pasta "al dente" (firm to the bite), mix it with the sauce and serve it immediately.

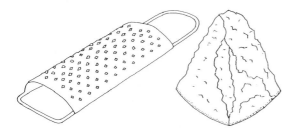

2nd method

In a bowl blend grated cheese, olive oil, cream, egg yolk(s), (warm) bechamel sauce, salt and pepper.

3rd method

In a saucepan warm up oil or butter, over low heat. Add cream or milk, and later on some grated cheese.

Dissolve the cheese in the sauce and add grated nutmeg (or lemon juice, chives or parsley).

The bain marie method ("double-boiler" method, "a bagnomaria")

The bain marie method of warming the food denotes the use of a water bath either for keeping the cooked food warm or for cooking without allowing the ingredients to be in direct contact with the heat of the stove. It usually implies the use of two pots, one with the water, the other with the food (a sauce or something else).

Preparation:

Dice the cheese (gor-gonzola or similar).

Melt some butter in a pot (over another larger pot with hot water).

Add some milk or cream and the diced cheese.

Mix for a minute or two and then add a couple of egg yolks, rapidly mixing.

Continue heating of the lower pot, letting the sauce to thicken. If necessary, add more milk.

At the and, season with freshly ground pepper.

Mixing,
without warming up

The cheese sauce can be prepared mixing fresh cheese, oil or melted butter, vegetables or aromatic herbs (finely chopped) for instance parsley, capers, onions, green olives, bell peppers, mustard, brandy.

Type of cheese to select: local hard cheese, grana padano, parmigiano reggiano, pecorino romano, gorgonzola, brie, mozzarella.

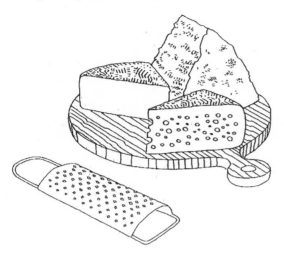

Optional ingredients: fresh cheese, ricotta cheese, olive oil, sage, minced prosciutto ham or pancetta, paprika, sweet wine, tomato purèe or passata, mint, chives, capers, salted anchovies, fried grated onions, pistachio, basil, worcester sauce, mustard, tabasco sauce, oregano, thyme, young onions, chopped and fried, walnuts, chopped finely, cream, vegetable bouillon powder.

PASTA
WITH GRATED CHEESE

Ingredients

pasta 400 g/14 oz
grated hard cheese
100-200 g/4-6 oz
olive oil 5-6 tbsp

Preparation

Mix the oil and the grated cheese in a bowl. Leave it to macerate for half an hour, at room temperature.

Cook the pasta in an abundant quantity of salted water.

Drain the pasta "al dente" (firm to the bite), mix it with the cheese sauce.

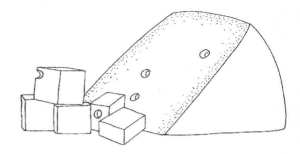

Optional ingredients: basil, parsley, paprika powder, salt, pepper.

PASTA
WITH FRESH CHEESE

Cook the short pasta in an abundant quantity of salted water. Drain it while it is still "al dente" (firm to the bite) and return it to the warm pot.

Add the fresh cheese, as much as you like, a couple of eggs, minced parsley leaves, salt and pepper. Put the pot on the stove and stir carefully, only for a minute, over low heat.

Optional ingredients: cooking cream, sour cream, butter, olive oil, mozzarella, curd, dried bacon, garlic, basil, oregano, capers, hard cheese.

PASTA WITH FRESH CHEESE, EGGS AND CREAM

Warm up a couple of tablespoons of olive oil and pour in the cooking cream (2 dl).

Continue cooking over low heat, until the cream becomes thickened.

Then remove the pan from the heat and stir in a couple of fresh eggs, the fresh cheese (10-30 dag), and salt and pepper, maybe even some milk.

PASTA WITH GRATED CHEESE AND EGG YOLKS

Cook the pasta in an abundant quantity of salted water. Drain it while it is still "al dente" (firm to the bite), add four egg yolks and grated cheese, 10-15 dag. Season with salt and pepper, and maybe even with finely chopped parsley leaves.

PASTA WITH GRATED CHEESE AND CREAM

Ingredients

pasta 400 g/14 oz
cooking cream 150-250 ml
olive oil or butter 2-3 tbsp
grated hard cheese
100-200 g/4-6 oz
nutmeg
salt

Preparation

Cook the pasta in an abundant quantity of salted water. Drain it while it is still "al dente" (firm to the bite), add oil or butter, cooking cream, grated cheese, grated nutmeg and salt. Pour in some of the remaining cooking water, not much.

Odabir tjestenine

Tagliatelle, spaghetti, farfalle (bow tie pasta), tortellini, fusilli, penne.

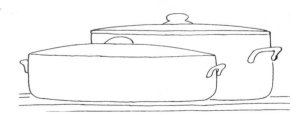

Optional ingredients

Gorgonzola, mozzarella, fresh cheese, sour cream, soft cheese, black olives, braised champignon mushrooms, fried diced dried bacon, chives, egg yolks, cooked peas, milk, cooked ham, lemon zest, peperoncino, parsley, basil, thyme, tomato passata, oregano, rucola, capers, almonds, cinnamon, paprika, beaten eggs.

PASTA WITH SHRIMPS AND ZUCCHINI

Ingredients

pasta 400 g/14 oz
cream 100-200 ml/ ½-1cup
shrimp tails 300-500 g/ 10 oz — 1 lb
olive oil 3-4 tbsp
garlic 1-2 cloves
zucchini 2-4
salt, pepper

Preparation

Wash and cut the zucchini into (rather small) cubes. Cook them for 1-2 minutes in salted water and then drain them. Chop the garlic.

In a saucepan warm up some olive oil and briefly fry the garlic, over low heat. Add the shrimp tails (fresh or frozen), and soon after that also the zucchini. Stir a couple of times and then let it all simmer for a few minutes, over medium heat. Eventually stir in the cream and season with salt and pepper.

Cook the pasta in an abundant quantity of salted water.

Drain the pasta "al dente", add it in-

to the simmering sauce, toss it for a minute or two over medium heat and serve it promptly.

Optional ingredients: scampi tails instead of shrimp tails, mint, cognac (brandy), dry white wine, vegetable bouillon powder, tomato paste, parsley, chili peppers, saffron, onions, shallots.

Possible omissions: garlic or cream.

SEAFOOD PASTA

Ingredients

pasta 400 g/14 oz
unshelled scampi or shrimp tails
500 g/1 lb
dry white wine
100-200 ml/ ½ - 1 cup
clams and/or mussels 1 kg/2 lb
tomato paste 1-2 tsp
bread crumbs 1 tbsp
olive oil 4-5 tbsp
garlic 1-3 cloves
salt, pepper
parsley

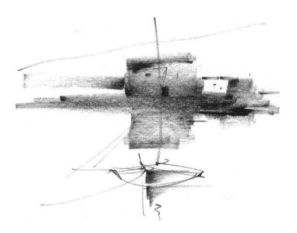

Preparation

Heat up the clams and/or mussels in pot, adding no water. When the shells open up, extract the meat, saving the salt water, i.e. the sea-water released by the mussels.

In a saucepan warm up some oil. Put in the chopped garlic and parsley. Let them fry over low heat for a while, but not long. Then add the bread crumbs and continue frying for a minute or two, still over low heat. Pour the wine and let it partly evaporate. After that, add the prepared seafood and the preserved liquid.

Continue cooking for another 15-20 minutes, stirring periodically. Add some water if necessary.

Season with salt and pepper.

Cook the pasta in an abundant quantity of salted water.

Drain the pasta "al dente", add it into the seafood sauce, toss it for a minute or two over medium heat and serve it promptly.

Optional herbs and spices: fried onions, desalted anchovy fillets, capers, bay leaves, paprika powder, sage, basil, lemon zest and juice, cognac (brandy), celery, carrots, chili peppers, chives.

Possible omissions: tomatoes, either shellfish or crab tails, wine.

PASTA WITH SALTED ANCHOVIES

Ingredients

pasta 400 g/14 oz
desalted anchovy fillets 20-40
olive oil 2-3 tbsp

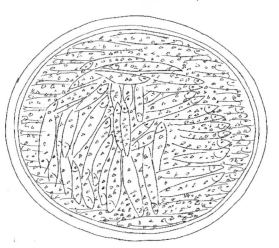

Preparation

In a saucepan warm up the oil. Add the anchovy fillets and let them dissolve over very low heat. As soon as it happens, immediately remove the pan from the heat.

Cook the pasta in an abundant quantity of salted water. Drain it "al dente" and season it with anchovy sauce. Serve right away or later.

Optional herbs and spices: parsley, soft inside of a bread slice, cut into smal cubes, and later fried in some oil, fried onions, wild fennel leaves, bread crumbs, tomato paste, pine nuts, raisins, garlic, basil, capers, green or blacka olives, thyme, celery, oregano, chili peppers, vegetable bouillon powder, rosemary, bay leaves, lemon zest and juice, vinegar, paprika powder, balsamic vinegar, red o dry white wine, cream, orange juice.

Optional proceeding: Add some liquid preserved after the cooking of the pasta.

PASTA
WITH TUNA FISH

Ingredients

pasta 400 g/14 oz
canned tuna fish 250 g /8 oz
olive oil 3-5 tbsp
cream 4-6 oz
salt, pepper

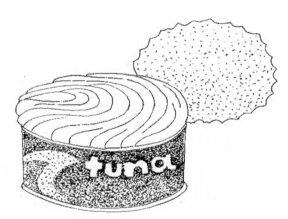

Preparation

Roughly mash the (already drained) tuna fish and add the cream, olive oil, salt and pepper.

Cook the pasta in an abundant quantity of salted water. Drain the pasta "al dente" (firm to the bite) and season with the tuna sauce.

Optional ingredients: canned or fried mushrooms, chopped and drained tomatoes, mozzarella cheese, (canned) artichokes, cooked vegetables (peas, corn, green peppers, cauliflower, broccoli), scampi or shrimp tails (cooked),

Optional herbs and spices: capers, garlic, parsley, dried tomatoes, tomato paste, sugar, dry white wine, oregano, mint, basil, thyme, onions, wild fennel, lemon zest and juice, vegetable bouillon powder, rosemary, bay leaves, black or green olives, desalted anchovy fillets, pine nuts, "pesto alla genovese" sauce, grated cheese, carrots, almonds, mayonnaise, pickled gherkins.

PASTA
WITH BASIL
AND PINE NUT PESTO

Ingredients

pasta 400 g/14 oz
grated hard cheese 7-8 tbsp
basil leaves 50 g/2 oz
olive oil 4-5 tbsp
garlic 1-3 cloves
pine nuts 1 tbsp
salt

eat and love Croatia

Preparation

Grind the garlic and the salt in a mortar. Then add the basil (not all at once), using circular motions. Later on, add the pine kernels and the cheese. Grind and mix well. Then pour in the oil, little by little, blending it in.

Cook the pasta in an abundant quantity of salted water.

Drain the pasta "al dente", season it with the sauce (pesto) and serve it.

Optional ingredients: walnuts instead of pine kernels.

Suggestion: To prepare the pesto use a marble mortar and a wooden pestle.

The use of a blender or a food processor will give results that can be evaluated only as acceptable, certainly not just as good.

Note: A "pesto" is a mixture of crushed ingredients, prepared primarily in order to season pasta.

The basil is highly esteemed as a seasoning. Its name in fact comes from the greek word "basilicon", meaning "*royal*".

The pine nuts (pine kernels) are the seeds of some species of pines.

PASTA WITH RED SAUCE

Ingredients

pasta 400 g/14 oz
ripe (plum) tomatoes 500 g/1 lb
brown or vegetable stock 2 cups
paprika powder 1-2 tsp
olive oil 4-5 tbsp
flour 1-2 tsp
sugar 1 tsp
onion 1
salt

Preparation

Peel the tomatoes and cut them into small pieces. Mince the onion.

Warm up the oil in a saucepan and fry the onion, over low heat. Then put in the tomatoes.

Cook for 5-10 minutes over medium heat. After that, pour in the stock and continue cooking for another 10-15 minutes, still over medium heat.

Filter the sauce and then add the flour (already melted in some water). Cook for 5-6 minutes, still over rather low heat. Then sparingly season the sauce with paprika powder, sugar and salt.

Cook the pasta in an abundant quantity of salted water.

Drain the pasta "al dente", add it into the sauce and serve it promptly.

Optional primary ingredients: red peppers.

Optional herbs and spices: peperoncino chili peppers, garlic, vinegar, dry white wine.

Note: The stock is a flavoured liquid base for making a sauce. A *white stock* is prepared by placing the ingredients directly into the water. In a *brown stock* the ingredients are first browned in fat and then the liquid is added. Stocks can be used in thickened or unthickened form.

Stocks can be based on vegetables, fish, veal, beef, bones, poultry or game, accompanied by aromatic herbs.

PASTA WITH TOMATO AND BELL PEPPER SAUCE

Ingredients

pasta 400 g/14 oz
ripe (plum) tomatoes 1 kg/2 lb
peperoncino chili peppers 1-2
bell peppers 1-3
vinegar 2-3 tbsp
olive oil 3-4 tbsp
garlic 1-3 cloves
sugar 1-2 tbsp
carrots 1-2
onions 1-2
salt

Preparation

Mince the onion, garlic and peperoncino chili peppers. Peel the tomatoes and peppers. Cut them into small pieces. Grate the carrots.

Warm up the oil in a saucepan. Fry the onion, over low heat. Add the garlic and carrot.

Mix a few times and then put the tomatoes in. Stir in some chopped peperoncino chili peppers and season with salt.

eat and love Croatia

Cover the pan and increase the heat to medium high, bringing the tomatoes to a low simmer. Cook for half an hour. Then season with the sugar and vinegar. Continue cooking for another 1.5-2 hours, over medium or even low heat.

Cook the pasta in an abundant quantity of salted water.

Drain the pasta "al dente", add it into the sauce and serve it promptly.

Optional herbs and spices: celery, sage, rosemary, basil, bay leaves, ground pepper.

Optional ingredients at the end: cinnamon, mustard.

Possible omissions: peperoncino chili peppers, vinegar, garlic.

Suggestions: The bell pepper sauce can also be served with polenta or slices of toasted bread, or it may accompany boiled meat.

PASTA WITH TOMATO AND EGGPLANT SAUCE

Ingredients

pasta 400 g/14 oz
yellow or/and red bell peppers 1-2
ripe tomatoes 500-800 g/1-2 lb
desalted anchovy fillets 3-5
green olives 1-2 oz
olive oil 4-5 tbsp
garlic 1-3 cloves
capers 1-3 tbsp
eggplants 1-3
salt, pepper
basil

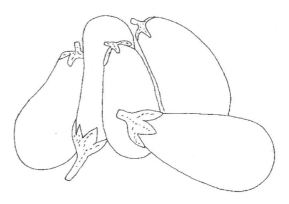

Preparation

Peel the tomatoes and dice them. Mince the capers and the anchovy fillets. Seed the bell peppers and cut them into short strips. Chop the olives. Mince finely the garlic. Chop the basil.

Peel the eggplants and cut them into small cubes. Sprinkle them with some salt and allow the eggplants to rest for half an hour, or an hour, to loose the bitter juices. Then rinse the eggplants and let them drain off.

Warm up oil in a pan and briefly fry the garlic, over low heat. Add eggplants and increase the heat. A couple of minutes later, add also the tomatoes and peppers. Continue cooking over moderate heat for another 15-20 minutes. Then put in anchovies, capers, olives, basil, salt and pepper. Let it simmer for a few minutes, turn down the heat and remove the pan.

Cook the pasta in an abundant quantity of salted water.

Drain the pasta "al dente", firm to the bite, mix it with the sauce and serve it immediately.

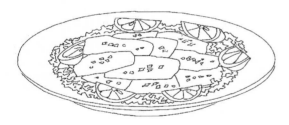

Optional ingredients: zucchini, onions.

Optional ingredients at the end: ricotta cheese, grated cheese, fried eggplant slices.

PASTA WITH TOMATO AND BACON SAUCE

Ingredients

pasta (bucatini or spaghetti) 400 g/14 oz

pancetta (dried bacon) 100-150 g/3-6 oz
tomatoes 250-350 g/8-12 oz
grated cheese 50 g/2 oz
olive oil 2-3 tbsp
salt, pepper
onion 1

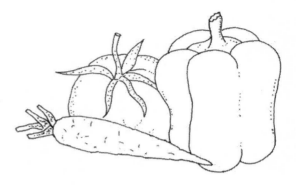

Preparation

Dice the pancetta (or bacon) and mince the onion. Peel the tomatoes and cut them into small pieces.

Fry the pancetta for a minute or two, in warm oil, and then add the minced onion. Continue frying over low heat for a couple of minutes. Then put in the tomatoes. Cook over medium heat until the liquid, contained in the tomatoes, evaporates. Season with salt and pepper and add some grated cheese. Stir a couple of times.

Cook the pasta in an abundant quantity of salted water.

Drain the pasta "al dente" (firm to the bite), mix it with the sauce and serve it immediately.

Optional herbs and spices: peperoncino chili peppers (instead of pepper), dry white whine, basil.

Possible omissions: onion or tomatoes.

Optional proceeding: Fry the diced pancetta separately and add it to the sauce a few moments before removing it from the heat.

PASTA WITH HERB SAUCE

Ingredients

pasta 400 g/14 oz
selected aromatic herbs
olive oil 4-5 tbsp
salt

Preparation

Cook the pasta, drain it and then season it with a herb sauce, already prepared.

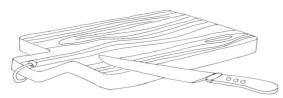

The herb sauce can be prepared by by mincing, chopping, crushing, mashing, whipping, whisking and/or beating aromatic herbs with a knife, or kitchen scissors, with a mortar and a (wooden) pestle, with an immersion blender (stick mixer), or with a food processor, possibly subsequently frying the minced herbs, over low heat, adding oil or butter and some salt, and/or, in some instances, blending them with other additional ingredients also.

Select one, two or more of the appropriate aromatic herbs: garlic, green onions, onions, basil, parsley, capers, sage, marjoram, chives, rosemary, shallots, bay leaves, thyme, oregano, mint, rocket salad, celery, carrots, chili peppers, pepper, saffron.

Other ingredients

Tomatoes (raw, paste, passata), cream, green or black olives, dry white wine, red wine, sweet wine, cognac (brandy), vinegar, balsamic vinegar (aceto balsamico), lemon zest and juice, orange zest and juice, concentrated meat, fish, crab or vegetable soup, sour cream, desalted anchovy fillets, egg yolks, cheese, leeks, mayonnaise, pancetta (dried bacon), prosciutto ham, bell peppers, prunes, mushrooms, raisins, almonds, walnuts, cinnamon, paprika powder, pine nuts, sugar, mustard, bread crumbs, pickled gherkins, nutmeg, honey, tabasco sauce, worcestershire sauce, the soft inside part of a bread slice, milk.

Note: By mixing the above mentioned herbs and ingredients it is possible to achieve thousands of successful combinations. Choose your own favorites.

Warning: Do not put too many different herbs and spices into the sauce. Add the seasonings gradually, tasting the sauce more than once in order to balance the flavours.

PASTA WITH TOMATOES AND OLIVES

Ingredients

spaghetti pasta 400 g/14 oz
ripe tomatoes 500 g/1 lb
black olives 3-5 oz
olive oil 4-5 tbsp
garlic 1-2 cloves
capers 1 tbsp
chili peppers
parsley
salt

Preparation

Cut the tomatoes into small pieces. Chop the capers, parsley, garlic, olives and chili peppers.

In a saucepan fry the parsley, garlic, olives and capers, shortly and over low heat. Soon add the tomatoes

and cook for 10-20 minutes over medium heat.

Cook the pasta in an abundant quantity of salted water. Drain the pasta "al dente" (firm to the bite), mix it with the sauce and the chili peppers and serve it immediately.

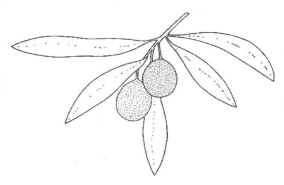

Optional ingredients: desalted anchovy fillets, tomato paste, oregano, sugar.

Possible omissions: chili peppers.

PASTA WITH VEGETABLES

Ingredients

pasta 400 g/14 oz
green beans 100-150 g/3-5 oz
pancetta (dried bacon) 50-100 g/2-3 oz
peas 100-150 g/3-5 oz
olive oil 4-5 tbsp
zucchini 1-3
salt, pepper
celery 1 rib
onions 1-2
carrot 1
basil

Preparation

Cut the zucchini, green beans and carrot into pieces. Dice the bacon in-

eat and love Croatia

to small cubes. Mince the onions, celery and basil.

Warm up the oil in a pan and gently fry the onions, over low heat. A minute or two later, add bacon, carrot and celery. Stir a few times, and then put in the peas, zucchini and green beans. Season with salt and pepper.

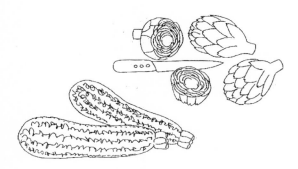

Continue cooking for 10-15 minutes over medium heat, stirring often. After that remove the pan from the heat and add some coarsely chopped basil leaves.

In the meantime, cook the pasta in an abundant quantity of salted water. Drain the pasta "al dente", firm to the bite, mix it with the sauce and serve it immediately.

Optional primary ingredients: green or red bell peppers, leeks (the white part), artichokes, tomatoes, mushrooms, (fried) eggplants, potatoes, asparagus, shrimps, ham, desalted anchovy fillets, pine nuts, canned tuna, green or black olives, shrimp or scampi tails.

Optional herbs and spices: capers, vegetable powder bouillon, various fresh aromatic herbs, chili powder, dry white wine, cream, garlic, marjoram, oregano, parsley, lemon zest and juice.

Optional ingredients at the end: grated cheese, ricotta cheese, mozzarella.

Possible omissions: bacon, green beans, peas.

Optional proceeding: Boil the vegetables o fry them before further use.

Different method: Season the pasta with grilled vegetables (eggplants, zucchini, tomatoes, bell peppers ...).

PASTA WITH TOMATOES, MUSHROOMS AND PEAS

Ingredients

pasta tagliatelle (green or not)
400 g/14 oz
mushrooms (champignon or others)
250-350 g/ 8-12 oz
dry white wine 100 ml/ ½ cup
tomatoes 200-400 g/7-14 oz
peas 200-400 g/7-14 oz
pancetta (dried bacon)
100-150 g/3-5 oz
olive oil 4-5 tbsp
salt, pepper
celery 1 rib
carrot 1
nutmeg
onion 1

Preparation

Clean and slice the mushrooms. Dice the bacon. Chop the onion, celery and carrot.

Warm up the oil and gently fry the chopped onions, over low heat. After doing that, add the bacon, carrot and celery. Fry for a few minutes over moderate heat and then put in the tomatoes. Later on add mushrooms also. Season with salt, pepper and grated nutmeg.

Continue cooking for another 15-20 minutes, still over medium heat. Pour in the wine and let it almost evaporate. After that add the peas.

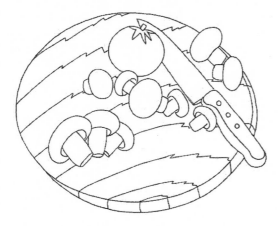

Continue cooking as long as necessary (pour some water when needed) and then remove the pan from the heat.

Cook the pasta in an abundant quantity of salted water.

Drain the pasta "al dente" (firm to the bite), mix it with the sauce and serve it immediately.

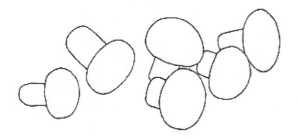

Optional herbs and spices: vegetable powder bouillon, cream, ham.

Optional ingredients at the end: grated cheese.

Possible omissions: wine, tomatoes, peas, celery, nutmeg or carrot.

PASTA WITH MUSHROOMS

Ingredients

pasta 400 g/14 oz
mushrooms (champignon, porcini or others) 300-800 g/10-25 oz
cream 100-250 g/3-7 oz
olive oil 3-4 tbsp
salt

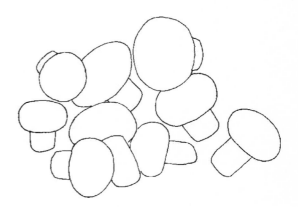

Preparation

Clean the mushrooms and slice them thinly.

Braise the mushrooms with some oil, over moderate heat, stirring often.

Let most of the liquid evaporate. Right after that remove the mushrooms from the heat.

Cook the pasta in an abundant quantity of salted water.

Drain the pasta and mix it with the mushroom sauce, joining also the cream, and serve it immediately.

Optional primary ingredients: milk instead of cream, tomatoes, black or green olives, (minced) meat, yellow bell peppers, leeks, peas, chicken livers, zucchini, canned tuna, artichokes, scampi o shrimp tails, dry white wine, dried mushrooms, ham, black olives, sausages.

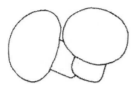

Optional herbs and spices: pepper, garlic, onions, parsley, cognac, chili peppers, vegetable powder bouillon, shallots, green onions, sausages, carrots, mint, thyme, pancetta (dried bacon), eggs, egg yolks, cooked eggs, tomatoes, oregano, celery, paprika powder, bechamel sauce, bay leaves, sage, cheese, ricotta cheese, chives, capers, marjoram, basil, sugar, rosemary, rocket salad, nutmeg, red or white wine, sweet wine, lemon zest and juice, pine nuts, vinegar, sour cream, desalted anchovy fillets, bread crumbs, peperoncino chili peppers, mustard.

Optional ingredients at the end: grated cheese, arugula, parsley, olives.

Possible omissions: cream.

PASTA WITH YOLKS, PANCETTA AND GRATED CHEESE

Ingredients

pasta 400 g/14 oz
(spaghetti, tagliatelle, bucatini)
pancetta (dried bacon)
or prosciutto ham
150-300 g /5-10 oz

grated hard cheese
(parmigiano o grana)
60-120 g/2-4 oz
olive oil 1-3 tbsp
egg yolks 4-6
salt, pepper

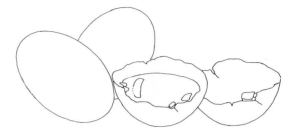

Preparation

Warm up the oil in a pan and then put in the diced (not very dry) pancetta, or even better the pork cheek dried bacon. Fry for a couple of minu-tes over medium heat, stirring all the time, until the pancetta becomes moderately crisp.

The yolks (four to six), or two yolks and two whole eggs (or three yolks and a whole egg, or two yolks and a whole egg, or three or four whole eggs, or four whole eggs and two yolks) beat lightly in a bowl, with a fork. Add one half of the prepared grated cheese (parmigiano reggiano, grana padano or pecorino romano, or use a combination of these cheeses), pepper (ground at the moment) and the pancetta, still warm.

Add a grain of salt, if necessary.

Use the sauce at the very moment the pasta is still very hot, having been just drained.

Pour in the seasoned pasta a tablespoon or two of the hot water remaining after draining the pasta, and also the grated cheese, earlier left behind to be used later.

Serve the pasta immediately.

Optional ingredients: cream, garlic (remove it as soon it starts changing its colour), finely chopped parsley, chili peppers (instead of pepper).

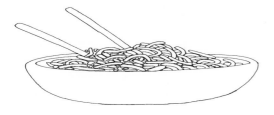

Optional proceeding: Cook the dry pancetta in water before dicing and frying it.

STUFFED PASTA

Ingredients

stuffed pasta (tortellini, ravioli, cappelletti o al.)
400 g/14 oz
grated cheese 50-80 g/2-3 oz
butter or olive oil 2-3 tbsp
cream 200 ml/7 oz
salt

Preparation

Cook the pasta in an abundant quantity of salted water. Drain the pasta "al dente" (firm to the bite), season it with cream, butter or oil, grated cheese and salt.

Note: The stuffed pasta, cooked and drained, may be seasoned with various sauces but those sauces which are light, of delicate flavour, are considered to be the most suitable.

BAKED PASTA

Ingredients

pasta 400 g/14 oz
selected sauce and/or aromatic herbs and spices
salt, pepper

Preparation

Cook the pasta in an abundant quantity of salted water. Drain the pasta very much "al dente" (a bit more undercooked than usual).

Grease the baking pan and line a layer of drained pasta on the bottom of the pan. Spread over it a layer of the selected sauce and the other ingredients.

Continue lining the layers of pasta and the layers of condiments. Top with bechamel sauce, tomato sauce, grated cheese or/and bread crumbs. Drizzle very lightly with olive oil.

Bake for 10-20 minutes in a preheated oven, at a rather high temperature.

eat and love Croatia

Allow the pasta to rest for a few minutes before serving it.

Pasta selection: maccheroni, bucatini, penne, rigatoni or other.

Sauce selection: ground meat sauce, cheese sauce, seafood sauce, mushroom sauce, vegetable sauce.

Optional ingredients: mortadella, tomatoes, cooked potatoes, prosciutto ham, mushrooms, cooked vegetables (peas, artichokes, eggplants, broad beans), cooked eggs, beaten eggs, cheese, desalted anchovy fillets, pancetta (dried bacon), bell peppers, ground meat, canned tuna.

Optional herbs and spices: onions, green onions, basil, chives, bechamel sauce, grated cheese, green or black olives, cream, parsley, chili peppers, nutmeg, garlic, oregano, celery, thyme, rosemary, marjoram, bay leaves, sage, dry white wine.

LASAGNE

Ingredients

dry lasagne pasta sheets 500 g
bechamel sauce
grated cheese
meat ragù

Preparation

Cook the pasta sheets in an abundant quantity of salted water. Drain the pasta very much "al dente" (undercooked).

Grease the baking pan and line a layer of drained pasta on the bottom of the pan. Spread over it the layers of ragù, bechamel sauce and grated cheese. Continue lining the layers of pasta and other ingredients. Top with bechamel sauce, tomato sauce and grated cheese. Drizzle very lightly with olive oil.

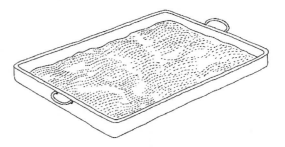

Bake for 20-40 minutes in a preheated oven, at a rather high temperature.

Allow the baked pasta ("lasagne alla bolognese") to rest for 5-10 minutes before serving it.

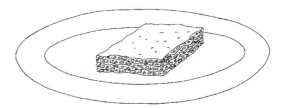

Optional ingredients: mushroom sauce, cheese sauce, cooked vegetables (artichokes, zucchini, green beans, peas, tomatoes, potatoes, eggplants or other), prosciutto ham, cheese (mozzarella or other).

Cannelloni

Cook the pasta sheets (drain it still somewhat undercooked). Spread over every sheet a relatively thin layer of the chosen filling (ragù, bechamel sauce, grated cheese, mushroom sauce or seafood sauce).

Roll up the filled pasta and then bake the cannelloni.

PASTA SALAD

Ingredients

short pasta 200-300 g
selected basic ingredients
and herbs and spices
olive oil 4-5 tbsp
salt, pepper

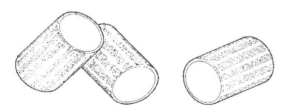

Preparation

The pasta salad (cold pasta) is prepared so that the boiled short pasta is left to slowly cool itself on room temperature, not in a refrigerator, and then seasoned with appropriate basic ingredients, herbs and spices.

Pasta selection: egg pasta (not exclusively), farfalle, penne, conchiglie, sedani, ditalini rigati, fusilli, pipe.

Optional basic ingredients

<u>Vegetables</u>: Salad tomatoes, mini tomatoes, leeks, radishes, salad, mushrooms, fried or grilled, boiled vegetables (peas, beans, green beans, corn, broad beans, chickpeas, carrots, broccoli, cowliflower), bell peppers, fresh, braised or grilled, arugula, pickles, cucumbers, fried eggplants.

<u>Meat</u>: dried bacon, boiled eggs, roast meat, mortadella, salami.

<u>Cheese</u>: Mozzarella, feta, parmesan, gran a or other.

<u>Seafood</u>: scampi or shrimp tails, squid, boiled or grilled, mussel meat, boiled cod, canned tuna fish, salted anchovies, boiled cuttlefish, boiled octopus, tinned sardines, smoked salmon.

<u>Herbs and spices</u>: green or black olives, olive oil, green onions, raisins, celery, cooking cream, almonds, walnuts, white vinegar, apple vinegar, (green) apples, aceto balsamico, basil, garlic, lemon juice and/or zest, oregano, capers, sugar, parsley, thyme, marjoram, paprika, chili pep-

eat and love Croatia

pers, onions, saffron, sage, rosemary, nutmeg, pesto alla genovese, salsa vinaigrette.

cheese, arugula, mozzarella, olives, yellow bell peppers, lemon zest and juice, onions, green onions, capers.

Avoid eccessive use of ingredients which can thicken the pasta salad too much, like grated cheese, soft cheese, vegetable puree.

Well-known pasta salads

Mediterannean pasta salad: short pasta, vegetables (salad tomatoes, bell peppers, zucchini, etc.), seafood (mussels, shrimps, scampi, cuttlefish etc.), green or black olives, basil, olive oil, salt, pepper.

Optional ingredients: lemon juice and zest, green onions, parsley.

Shepherd pasta salad: short pasta, salad tomatoes or mini tomatoes, mozzarella, mortadella, feta cheese, cooked ham, boiled eggs, parsley, salt, pepper.

Optional ingredients: green or black olives, salted anchovies, green onions, mayonnaise, worcester sauce.

Suggestions

The vegetables are not to be cut to a size larger than the size of the pasta.

Garden pasta salad: short pasta, salad tomatoes, bell peppers, zucchini, boiled peas, garlic, mozzarella, basil, olive oil, salt, pepper.

Optional ingredients: oregano, feta

Do not cool the boiled pasta by rinsing it. It will soak with water and eventually become limp and gummy.

Prepare the pasta salad not more than a couple of hours before consumption.

Meanwhile, do not keep it in the refrigerator.

COLD PASTA WITH CANNED TUNA AND OLIVES

Ingredients

short pasta 400 g
mini (cherry) tomatoes 10-15
tuna fish 2-3 cans
green olives 7-20
olive oil 3-4 tbsp
capers 1-3 tbsp
salt, pepper

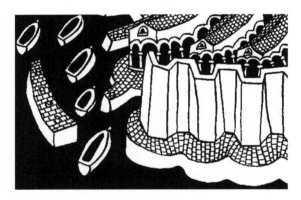

Preparation

Cook the pasta in an abundant quantity of salted water.

Drain the pasta "al dente" (firm to the bite), mix it with other ingredients and serve it cold later or immediately.

Optional ingredients: mozzarella, feta cheese, salted anchovies, black olives, boiled peas, arugula, parsley, oregano, lemon zest.

PASTA WITH A TASTY SAUCE

Ingredients

pasta 400 g
whole peeled (plum) tomatoes, fresh or tinned 250-500 g
bread crumbs 1 tsp
olive oil 4-5 tbsp
garlic 1-2 cloves
salt, pepper
cloves 1-2
rosemary
carrot 1
nutmeg
parsley
celery

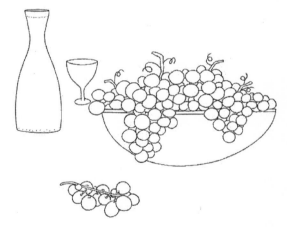

Preparation

Rinse and peel the carrot. Chop the garlic, parsley, rosemary and celery. Peel, slice and dice the tomatoes.

Warm up the oil in a casserole and then gently fry the chopped herbs, for a minute or two, stirring all the time. Then add the tomatoes. Continue cooking over medium heat. Season the sauce with cloves, rosemary, grated nutmeg, salt and pepper. Add a teaspoonful of bread

eat and love Croatia

crumbs. Continue the cooking, over medium heat, stirring often. Pour in some water from time to time. Use the sauce to season the pasta.

Optional ingredients: fresh sausage, dried bacon, vegetable bouillon pow-der or cube, dry white wine, dry plums, sugar, basil, marjoram.

WALNUT PASTA

Ingredients

pasta 400 g
butter or olive oil 4-5 tbsp
salt, pepper

Preparation

Warm up the oil or butter in a sau-cepan, over low heat. Then add the walnuts, previously ground.

Still over low heat, stir the walnuts in oil. Use the walnut sauce to sea-son the boiled and drained pasta. Spice up with salt and pepper.

2nd method

Gently fry the chopped onions with some crumbs, in oil or butter, over low heat. Then add the ground wal-nuts.

3rd method

Drain the boiled pasta and season it with butter or olive oil, adding the ground walnuts.

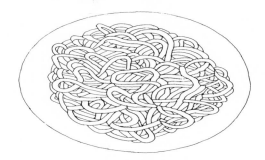

Optional ingredients: pine nuts, parsley, salt, pepper, sugar, honey.

FRESH SAUSAGE PASTA

Ingredients

pasta 400 g
cooking cream 100-200 ml
fresh sausages 400-700 g
olive oil 4-5 tbsp
salt, pepper
onions 1-3

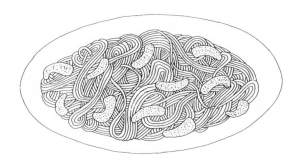

Preparation

Remove the casing from the fresh sausages and then cut the meat into 2-3 cm long pieces.

Warm up the oil in a pan and then gently fry the chopped onions, over low heat, until they turn pale gold.

Pour in the cooking cream and continue to cook the sauce for another 7-10 minutes, still over low heat. Season with salt and pepper.

Cook the pasta in an abundant quantity of salted water.

Drain the pasta "al dente" and season it with the fresh sausage sauce.

Optional ingredients: garlic, paprika, tomato paste or passata, basil, vegetable bouillon powder or cube, dry white wine, oregano, thyme and, before serving, grated hard cheese.

PASTA WITH CUTTLEFISH AND BROAD BEANS

Ingredients

pasta 400 g
broad beans (fresh or frozen) 150-300 g
dry white wine 100-150 ml
cuttlefish 300-500 g
olive oil 4-5 tbsp
garlic 2-3 cloves
salt, pepper
onions 1-2
parsley

Preparation

Clean and rinse the cuttlefish. Cut them to pieces. Peel the onions and garlic and chop them finely. Mince the parsley.

Warm up the oil in a pan and then gently fry the chopped onions, over low heat, until they turn pale gold.

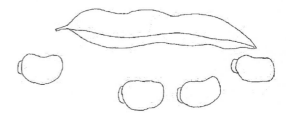

When that happens, add the garlic and parsley. Stir and put in the cuttlefish and broad beans. Continue cooking for half an hour.

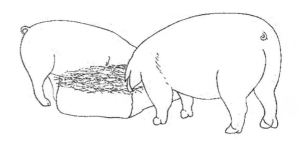

Cook the pasta (spaghetti or tagliatelle) in an abundant quantity of salted water.

Drain the pasta "al dente" and season it with the prepared sauce.

Optional ingredients: peas, artichokes, tomatoes, potatoes, dried bacon, mushrooms, beans, chickpeas.

Optional herbs and spices: saffron, wine, capers, basil.

Optional ingredients at the end: grated cheese, curd, fresh cheese.

Optional proceeding: Roll the meat pieces in flour, coating them lightly.

PASTA WITH MEAT AND MUSHROOMS

Ingredients

pasta 400 g
meat (veal, pork or chicken) 700 g – 1 kg
mushroooms (champignon, porcini or others) 250-500 g
cooking cream 100-200 ml
olive oil 4-5 tbsp
salt, pepper
flour

Preparation

Cut the meat into small pieces. Slice the mushrooms.

Optional ingredients: grated bell pepper, fresh eggs or yolks only, boiled eggs, green or black olives, tomatoes, leeks, boiled peas.

Optional herbs and spices: vegetable bouillon powder or cube, oregano, carrots, tomato paste, parsley, gorgonzola, sage, garlic, capers, thyme.

PASTA WITH FRIED MEAT BALLS

Ingredients

short pasta 400 g
minced meat (veal or pork) 700 g - 1 kg
vegetable or meat bouillon powder
the middle of two bread slices
dalmatian seasoning mix
dry white wine 100 ml
olive oil 7-8 tbsp
garlic 1-2 cloves
bread crumbs
salt, pepper
eggs 2-3
parsley

Preparation

Let the middle of two bread slices soak in water or milk for a few minutes. Then wring the bread, not too firmly.

Beat the eggs. Chop the garlic and the parsley leaves.

In a bowl mix the meat, bread, eggs, vegetable or meat bouillon powder, but not too much, garlic, parsley, salt, pepper and some bread crumbs.

Chopped green olives, sliced mushrooms or a suitable cheese can be added to the mixture.

Shape the meat balls, as big as cherries, and press them in bread crumbs (or in flour).

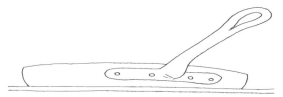

Fry the meat balls in oil and take them out when they are ready.

Pour the dry white wine into the remaining oil and then add the dalmatian seasoning mix, just a bit. Let the wine almost evaporate and then stir in some bread crumbs, but not much.

Cook the pasta in an abundant quantity of salted water. Drain the pasta "al dente" and season it with the prepared sauce. Also add the fried meat balls.

Optional ingredients for the sauce: tomato paste or passata, cooking cream, lemon zests, lemon thyme.

PASTA
WITH MEAT AND PEAS

Ingredients

pasta 400 g
meat (veal pork or chicken)
500 - 800 g
tomatoes 200-500 g
olive oil 4-5 tbsp
garlic 1-3 cloves
peas 300-500 g
salt, pepper
carrot 1
nutmeg
onion 1
parsley

Preparation

Cut the meat in pieces. Chop the tomatoes, onion, garlic and parsley. Grate the carrots.

Warm up the oil in a pan and then gently fry the chopped onions, over low heat, until they turn pale gold. Then add the meat and the peas. Stir in also all the other seasonings. Cook until the meat softens enough and then season the drained boiled pasta.

Optional ingredients: dried bacon, wine, lemon zests, vegetable or meat bouillon powder, cooking cream.

PASTA WITH FRESH TUNA

Ingredients

pasta (spaghetti) 400 g
fresh tuna meat 300-500 g
olive oil 4-5 tbsp
garlic 1-2 cloves
tomatoes 1-2
salt, pepper
parsley
flour

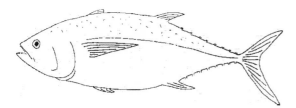

Preparation

Cut the tuna meat into cubes and roll them lightly in flour. Peel the tomatoes and cut them to pieces. Chop the garlic and parsley.

Warm up the oil and fry the garlic and parsley, only for a minute, stirring continuously over low heat. Soon add the tuna meat and the tomatoes. Keep on the slow cooking over medium heat for another 5-10 minutes. Add salt and pepper. Season the drained pasta with tuna sauce.

Optional ingredients: black or green olives, green beans, bell peppers, zucchini, shell meat, shrimp tail meat, leeks, salted anchovies, sweet or dry white wine, onions, chili peppers, lemon zest, bread crumbs, celery, bay leaves, capers, rosemary.

The sauce will become creamy if some of the tuna cubes are crushed at the end of the preparation.

PASTA IN BLACK

Ingredients

pasta (spaghetti, penne) 400 g
ripe tomatoes 1-2
olive oil 4-5 tbsp
garlic 2-3 cloves
cuttlefish 1 kg
salt, pepper
onions 1-2
parsley

This dalmatian dish got its name from the squid ink which paints the pasta into the black color.

Preparation

Clean the cuttlefish and cut its meat into pieces, not too small. Save the ink bags by putting them into a cup and diluting the ink with some water, fish broth, dry white wine or oil. Chop the onions, garlic and parsley.

In a saucepan fry the onions over low heat. Before long, add the garlic and parsley. Stir a couple of times and put in the cuttlefish and tomatoes.

Continue cooking over medium heat, adding some warm broth or water every now and then. Stir often. A couple of minutes before the end, add the diluted cuttlefish ink.

Season the drained pasta with the black cuttlefish sauce.

Optional primary ingredients: (yellow) bell peppers, tomato paste instead of fresh tomatoes, mussel meat, squid (calamari), scampi or shrimp tail meat, mushrooms, almonds, broad beans, peas.

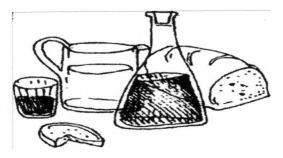

Optional herbs and spices: red or dry white wine, dessert wine, chili peppers, cognac (brandy), vinegar, balsamic vinegar (aceto balsamico), cream, lemon zest and juice, celery, thyme, basil, capers, sugar, rosemary, green or black olives, cheese, honey, vegetable bouillon powder, fish broth, desalted anchovy fillets.

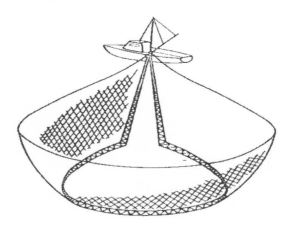

Optional ingredients at the end: grated cheese.

Possible omissions: tomatoes, cuttlefish ink.

FOOZI WITH TRUFFLES

Ingredients

pasta (foozi) 400 g
olive oil or butter 2-4 tbsp
white or black truffles 50-80 g
or
tartufata 80-160 g
salt, pepper

Preparation

Cook the pasta in an abundant quantity of salted water. Drain the pasta "al dente" and season it with some olive oil and butter, the grated mushrooms or with the tartufata sauce.

Optional ingredients: cooking cream, boiled shrimp or scampi meat, grated cheese, peperoncino.

Note: Foozi is the traditional Istrian homemade pasta.

Tartufata is a mixture of white truffles, black truffles, champignons, extra virgin olive oil, sunflower oil, salt, pepper.

eat and love Croatia

RICE

RISI BISI
(RICE AND PEAS)

Ingredients

rice 200-300 g / 7-10 oz
pancetta (dried bacon)
50-80 g / 2-3 oz
vegetable broth 1 l / 1 quart
or
vegetable bouillon powder 1 tbsp
or
1 cube
grated cheese 3-5 tbsp
butter 30-50 g / 1-2 oz
olive oil 3-4 tbsp
peas 1 kg / 2 lb
salt, pepper
onion 1
parsley

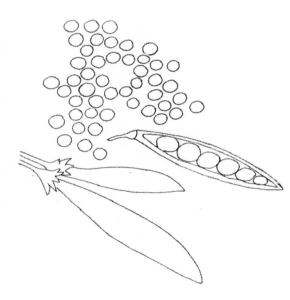

Preparation

In a pot warm up the oil. Gently fry the chopped onions, adding soon also the minced parsley, over low heat. Stir a few times and pour in the peas. Cover the pot and increase the heat to medium high.

After 2-3 minutes, stir in the rice (already separately fried with some oil for a minute or two).

Continue cooking over medium heat, adding some warm broth or water every now and then. Stir often. Season with salt and pepper.

Cook the rice until it is tender, but still firm to the bite. Off heat, stir in the butter and the grated cheese. Serve after a couple of minutes of rest.

Optional primary ingredients: ground meat, mushrooms, broad beans, leeks, tomatoes, artichokes, green beans, cuttlefish, scampi or shrimp tails, canned tuna, zucchini, green onions.

Optional herbs and spices: garlic, ham, bread crumbs, tomato paste, chives, green onions, mint, nutmeg, carrots, cream, vegetable bouillon powder, cloves, marjoram, chili peppers, basil, celery, lemon zest and juice, capers, dry white wine.

Optional ingredients at the end: parsley, mint, grated cheese, ricotta, eggs beaten with lemon zest and juice.

Possible omissions: garlic, pancetta (dried bacon) or onions.

Suggestions: The dish need not be as dry as a normal risotto. It may have the density of a rather dense vegetable soup.

Optional proceeding: Pea pods (green), cooked and mashed into puré, may also be included, before adding the rice.

Different method: Cook the peas and the rice separately and then mix them together.

VEGETABLE RISOTTO

Ingredients

rice 250-350 g / 8-11 oz
pancetta (dried bacon)
60-150 g / 2-5 oz
broad beans 100-200 g / 3-7 oz
peas 100-200 g / 3-7 oz
olive oil 4-5 tbsp
ripe tomato 1
salt, pepper
celery rib 1
zucchini 1
carrot 1
onion 1
parsley
butter

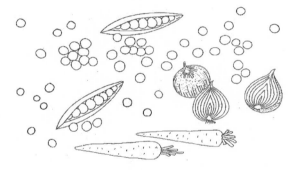

Preparation

In a saucepan warm up the oil. Fry chopped onions over low heat. Then add the diced pancetta, stir a couple of times and proceed with adding (one by one) all the vegetables, already cut to pieces. Cook for 5-6 minutes over medium heat.

Stir in the rice (already separately fried with some oil for a minute or two).

Continue cooking over medium heat, adding some warm broth or water every now and then. Stir often. Season with salt and pepper.

Cook the rice until it is tender, but still firm to the bite. Off heat, stir in the butter and the chopped parsley. Serve after a couple of minutes of rest.

Optional primary ingredients: artichokes, eggplants, potatoes, leeks, green beans, bell peppers, mushrooms, red lentils, tomatoes, green onions, scampi or shrimp tails, cauliflower, corn, cooked beans.

Optional herbs and spices: garlic, vegetable bouillon powder, sage, basil, wild fennel, chili peppers, bay leaves, red or dry white wine, lemon zest or juice, saffron, black or green olives, marjoram, thyme, capers, nutmeg, paprika powder, rosemary, sweet wine.

Optional ingredients at the end: grated cheese, rocket salad, green onions, garlic, parsley, cream.

Possible omissions: pancetta or celery.

Riso e verdure
(rice and vegetables)

Cook separately the rice and each of the chosen vegetables. Mix all the cooked and afterwards drained ingredients. Season with salt, pepper, butter and other condiments.

eat and love Croatia

MUSHROOM RISOTTO

Ingredients

rice 250-350 g / 8-11 oz
cream 50-80 ml / 2-3 oz
mushrooms 500 g / 1 lb
olive oil 4-5 tbsp
salt, pepper
butter

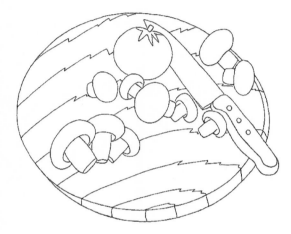

Preparation

Clean, briefly rinse and then thinly slice the mushrooms.

Braise the mushrooms with some oil, over moderate heat, stirring often. Let most of the liquid evaporate. Right after that, stir in the rice (already separately fried for a minute or two, with some oil).

Continue cooking over medium heat, adding some warm broth or water every now and then. Stir often.

Cook the rice until it is tender, but still firm to the bite. Minute or two before the end, add the cream. Off heat, stir in the butter. Season with

salt and pepper. Serve after a couple of minutes of rest.

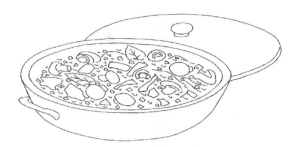

Optional primary ingredients: milk instead of cream, (ground) meat, artichokes, bell peppers, peas, chicken livers, leeks, shrimp or scampi tails, dry mushrooms.

Optional herbs and spices: vegetable bouillon powder, garlic, parsley, chili peppers, shallots, carrots, green onions, eggs, egg yolks, cooked eggs, pancetta (dried bacon), chives, tomatoes, oregano, celery, paprika powder, saffron, marjoram, bay leaves, (fresh) cheese, ricotta cheese, capers, sage, basil, thyme, mint, sugar, rosemary, nutmeg, black or green olives, red or dry white wine, lemon zest, sweet wine, vinegar, bechamel sauce, sour cream, mustard.

Optional ingredients at the end: grated cheese.

BELL PEPPER RISOTTO

Ingredients

rice 250-350 g / 8-11 oz
yellow bell pepper 1
green bell pepper 1

ripe tomatoes 1-2
red bell pepper 1
olive oil 4-5 tbsp
garlic 1-2 cloves
onions 1-2
butter
salt

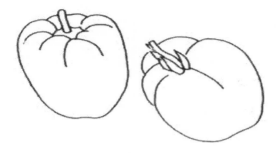

Preparation

Cut the bell peppers into small cubes. Chop finely the onions and garlic. Peel the tomatoes and cut them into small pieces.

In a saucepan warm up the oil and fry the onions, over low heat. Then increase the heat and add the rice. Let it fry for a minute or two. Stir constantly. After that, add the bell peppers and tomatoes.

Continue cooking over medium heat, adding some warm broth or water every now and then, when needed. Stir often. Season with salt and pepper.

Cook the rice until it is tender, but still firm to the bite. Off heat, stir in the butter. Serve after a couple of minutes of rest.

Optional primary ingredients: zucchini, black or green olives, canned tuna, sausages.

Optional herbs and spices: dry white wine, cream, pancetta (dried bacon), parsley, vegetable bouillon powder, basil, capers, oregano, rosemary, thyme, bay leaves.

Optional ingredients at the end: grated cheese.

Possible omissions: tomatoes, onions or garlic.

Different method: Mix the separately cooked rice and the gently fried bell peppers (with o without garlic, onions and/or tomatoes). Add butter or oil, season with salt and pepper.

BLACK RISOTTO

Ingredients

rice 250-350 g / 8-11 oz
cuttlefish 1 kg / 2 lb
ripe tomatoes 1-2
olive oil 4-5 tbsp
garlic 2-3 cloves
salt, pepper
onions1-2
parsley
butter

This popular dalmatian dish got its name from the squid ink which paints it in black.

Preparation

Clean the cuttlefish and cut its meat into pieces, not too small. Save the ink bags by putting them into a cup and diluting the ink with some water, fish broth, dry white wine or oil. Chop the onions, garlic and parsley.

In a saucepan fry the onions over low heat. Before long, add the garlic and parsley. Stir a couple of times and put in the cuttlefish and tomatoes. Cook for a few minutes over medium heat and then stir in the rice (already separately fried for a minute or two, with some oil).

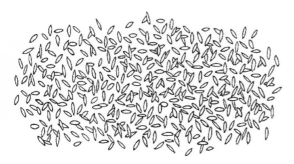

Continue cooking over medium heat, adding some warm broth or water every now and then. Stir often. A couple of minutes before the end, add the diluted cuttlefish ink.

Cook the rice until it is tender, but firm to the bite. Off heat, stir in the butter. Serve after a couple of minutes of rest.

Optional primary ingredients: (yellow) bell peppers, tomato paste instead of fresh tomatoes, squid (calamari), clam or mussel meat, scampi or shrimp tail meat, mushrooms, almonds, broad beans, peas.

Optional herbs and spices: red or dry white wine, dessert wine, chili peppers, cognac (brandy), vinegar, balsamic vinegar (aceto balsamico), cream, lemon zest and juice, celery, thyme, basil, capers, sugar, rosemary, green or black olives, cheese, honey, vegetable bouillon powder, fish broth, desalted anchovy fillets.

Optional ingredients at the end: grated cheese.

Possible omissions: cuttlefish ink, tomatoes.

TOMATO RISOTTO

Ingredients

rice 250-350 g / 8-11 oz
ripe tomatoes 500 g — 1 kg/ 1-2 lb
olive oil 3-4 tbsp
salt, pepper
sugar ½ tsp
onions 1-2
butter

Preparation

Peel the tomatoes and cut them into small pieces. Chop finely the onions.

In a saucepan warm up the oil and

fry the onions, over low heat. Then add the tomatoes. Increase the heat to medium and let the tomatoes cook for 5-10 minutes, stirring occasionally.

Stir in the rice (already separately fried with some oil for a minute).

Continue cooking over medium heat, adding some warm broth or water every now and then. Stir often. Season with salt and pepper.

Cook the rice until it is tender, but still firm to the bite. Off heat, stir in the butter. Serve after a couple of minutes of rest.

Optional herbs and spices: garlic, parsley, basil, carrot, cloves, celery, bay leaves, nutmeg, pancetta (dried bacon), dry white wine, prosciutto ham, sage, paprika powder, vegetable bouillon powder or cube.

Optional ingredients at the end: grated cheese, basil, parsley.

WHITE RISOTTO

Ingredients

rice 250-350 g / 8-11 oz
grated cheese
70-150 g / 2-5 oz
dry white wine
100-120 ml / ½ cup
olive oil 3-4 tbsp
salt, pepper
butter

Preparation

In a saucepan warm up the oil and then add the rice. Let it fry for no more than two minutes, stirring it constantly. After that, pour the wine and let it almost evaporate.

Continue cooking over medium heat, adding some warm broth or water every now and then, when needed. Stir often.

Cook the rice until it is tender, but firm to the bite. Off heat, stir in the cheese and butter. Season with salt and pepper. Serve after a couple of minutes of rest.

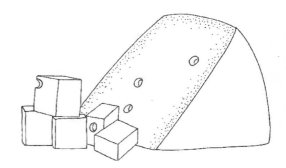

Optional herbs and spices: fried onions, green onions, shallots, nutmeg, vegetable bouillon powder, basil, parsley, orange juice, cream.

Possible omissions: dry white wine.

GROUND MEAT RISOTTO

Ingredients

rice 250-350 g / 8-11 oz
minced (beef or pork) meat
800 g / 2 lb
ripe (plum) tomatoes 500 g / 1 lb
tomato paste 1-2 tbsp
olive oil 4-5 tbsp
garlic 2-3 cloves
bay leaves 3-7
salt, pepper
onions 1-2
parsley

Preparation

In a saucepan fry the chopped onions, over low heat, adding soon also the chopped garlic and parsley. Then put in the meat and stir for a few minutes. After that add the tomatoes. Season with salt, pepper and bay leaves. Let the meat cook for approximately one hour. Then stir in the rice (already separately fried for a minute or two, with some oil).

Continue cooking over medium heat, adding some warm broth or water every now and then. Stir quite frequently.

Cook the rice until it is tender, but still firm to the bite. Season with salt and pepper. Serve after a couple of minutes of rest.

Optional herbs and spices: sausages, dry mushrooms, pancetta (dried bacon), prosciutto ham, red or dry white wine, celery, carrot, cloves, vegetable bouillon powder, sugar, nutmeg, lemon zest, basil, rosemary, cinnamon, milk.

Optional ingredients at the end: grated cheese, cream.

Possible omissions: garlic or parsley.

Different method: Mix the (already completely prepared) ragù with the rice only when it is almost cooked.

SCAMPI RISOTTO

Ingredients

rice 250-350 g / 8-11 oz
unshelled scampi (tails)
1-1,5 kg / 2-3 lb
cognac (armagnac, brandy)
1-2 tbsp
dry white wine 100 ml / ½ cup
bread crumbs 2 tbsp
tomato paste 1 tsp
olive oil 4-5 tbsp
garlic 2-3 cloves
salt, pepper
parsley

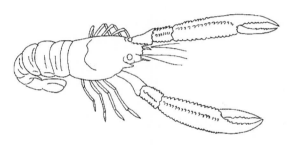

Preparation

In a pan warm up the oil. Gently fry the finely chopped garlic and parsley. Later on add the crumbs. Fry still over low heat, not more than a minute. Then add the scampi (tails). Stir a couple of times and pour in the wine. Add the tomato paste, as well as the salt and pepper. Pour also some water, taking care not to surpass the upper level of the ingredients in the pan. Add a tablespoon of cognac.

Continue cooking over medium heat, for 5-10 minutes. Then stir in the rice (already separately fried for a minute or two, with some oil). Keep cooking, stirring very often. Every now and then, add some warm fish broth (or the broth prepared with the discarded scampi body parts, intestines excluded), or warm water.

Cook the rice until it is tender, but still firm to the bite. Off heat, stir in the butter. Serve after a couple of minutes of rest.

Optional primary ingredients: cuttlefish, clam or mussel meat, (yellow) bell peppers, mushrooms, zucchini, peas, wild fennel, desalted anchovy fillets.

Optional herbs and spices: shallots, thyme, marjoram, paprika powder, vegetable bouillon powder, cloves, chili peppers, rosemary, pine nuts, almonds, bay leaves, lemon zest and/or juice, saffron, onions, green onions, sugar, sage, carrots, mustard, sweet wine, chives, celery.

Optional ingredients at the end: grated cheese, cream, arugula.

Note: The same recipe is also used for the preparation of the famous "seafood risotto" ("risotto ai frutti di mare") in which case the scampi should be accompanied by some clams or/and mussels, possibly also shrimp tail meat and perhaps even squid or cuttlefish meat.

SHRIMP RISOTTO

Ingredients

shelled shrimp (prawn) tail meat (fresh or frozen) 400-750 g
rice 250-350 g / 8-11 oz
olive oil 4-5 cucchiai
salt, pepper
lemons 1-3
onion 1
butter

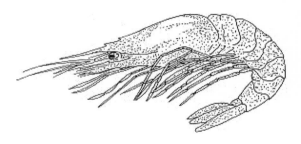

Preparation

In a pan fry the chopped onion, over low heat. Add the shelled shrimp tails and lemon zest. Stir a few times and pour in the rice (already separately fried with some oil for a minute or two). Continue cooking over medium heat, adding some warm broth or water every now and then. Stir often. Season carefully with salt and pepper.

Cook the rice until it is tender, but still firm to the bite. Off heat, stir in the butter. Serve after a couple of minutes of rest.

Optional ingredients: zucchini, vegetable bouillon powder or cube, garlic, parsley, bread crumbs, dry

eat and love Croatia

white wine, cognac (brandy), shallots, carrots.

Optional ingredients at the end: grated cheese, lemon juice, cream.

Possible omissions: lemon zest.

MUSSEL RISOTTO

Ingredients

fresh unshelled mussels
or
other type of shells
1,5-2 kg
rice 250-350 g / 8-11 oz
olive oil 4-5 cucchiai
garlic 1-2 cloves
bread crumbs
salt, pepper
parsley
butter

Preparation

In a large pan heat up the clams or/and mussels. Then extract the meat from the shells. Filtrate the liquid that has remained after that.

In a pan warm up some oil and gently fry the finely chopped parsley and garlic, over low heat. Soon add the bread crumbs and stir a few times. Then put the clam (mussel) meat, stir for a minute, and pour in the rice (already separately fried with some oil for a minute or two).

Continue cooking over medium heat, adding some warm preserved liquid every now and then. Stir often. Season with salt and pepper.

Cook the rice until it is tender, but still firm to the bite. Off heat, stir in the butter. Serve after a couple of minutes of rest.

Optional primary ingredients: zucchini, (yellow) bell peppers, broad beans.

Optional herbs and spices: tomato paste, dry white wine, chili peppers, fried onions, desalted anchovy fillets, black or green olives, cloves, marjoram, lemon zest and/or juice, basil, capers, oregano, chives, saffron.

Optional ingredients at the end: grated cheese, cream, rocket salad, egg yolks.

Possible omissions: wine, parsley.

RICE BALLS

Ingredients

Filling:

tomato paste 1-3 tbsp
ground (minced) meat
150-200 g / 5-7 oz
mozzarella cheese 150 g / 5 oz
red or dry white wine
100 ml / ½ cup
peas 80-100 g /3 oz
olive oil 5-6 tbsp
salt, pepper
butter 1 oz
onion 1

Rice:

rice 400-450 g / 1 lb
grated cheese 50 g / 2 oz
butter or olive oil 30 g / 1 oz
egg yolks 3
saffron

Coating:
bread crumbs
eggs 2

Frying:
frying oil

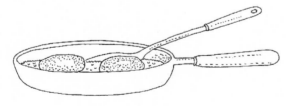

Preparation

In a pot warm up 1-25 quarts of salted water. Pour in the rice and let it cook. Drain the cooked rice and stir in the butter or oil, saffron, egg yolks and grated cheese.

Leave it to rest for a couple of hours.

In the meantime, cook the peas in a quart of water.

In a pan warm up the butter with the oil and the finely chopped onion, over low heat. Add the meat, increase the heat to medium, and fry for a minute or two, stirring constantly. Then pour in the wine and let it almost evaporate. Add the tomato paste and some water.

Continue cooking for 15-20 minutes over moderate heat. Season with salt and pepper. Remove the pan from the heat and stir in the cooked peas.

Cut the chosen cheese(s) into small cubes.

In the palm of a hand, flatten a small quantity of rice and form a circle, rather thin. In the center of the circle put a small quantity of the meat and pea filling and 1-2 cheese cubes.

Cover the filled rice with some more rice and form a small ball. Roll the rice balls in the beaten eggs and after that in the bread crumbs.

Fry the balls in an abundant quantity of oil, not many at the same time. A minute or two later, remove them from the oil and lay them on paper towels to drain the oil.

Optional primary ingredients for the meat: garlic, cloves, bay leaves, dry white instead of red wine, vegetable bouillon powder.

Optional proceeding: before rolling the balls in the eggs, roll them in flour.

Note: Instead of filling the rice balls with meat, fill them with cheese, prosciutto ham or ricotta cheese with spinach.

TUNA RICE SALAD

Ingredients

rice 200-250 g
yellow or red bell pepper 1
pickled gherkins 2-3
green olives 100 g
olive oil 4-5 tbsp
salad tomato 1
tuna fish 1 tin
salt, pepper
peas 100 g
lemon 1

Preparation

Cook the rice until it is tender, but still firm to the bite.

Rinse the boiled rice and transfer it into a bowl.

Stir in coarsely chopped green olives, boiled peas, tuna fish, chopped tomato and bell pepper, chopped pickled gherkins, lemon juice, lemon zest, olive oil, salt and pepper.

Optional ingredients: scampi or shrimp tail meat, slightly boiled, boiled cuttlefish or squid, boiled mussel meat, parsley, garlic, black olives, radishes, green onions, feta cheese, mozzarella, boiled eggs, desalted anchovy fillets, bell pepper.

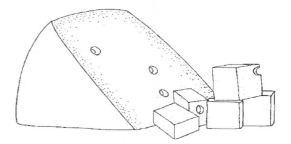

MORTADELLA AND CHEESE RICE SALAD

Ingredients: boiled rice, mozzarella or feta cheese, fresh cheese, salad tomatoes, capers, endivia salad, parsley, olive oil, salt, pepper.

SHRIMP AND ZUCCHINI RICE SALAD

Ingredients: boiled rice, zucchini, red and yellow bell peppers, cucumbers, parsley, carrots, lemon zests, green onions, olive oil, salt, pepper.

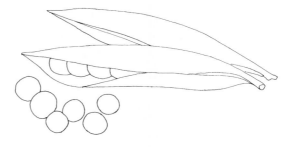

HAM AND PEAS RICE SALAD

Ingredients: boiled rice, ham, boiled peas, black olives, garlic, sugar, bell pepper, boiled eggs, lemon zests, salad tomatoes, basil or parsley, olive oil, salt, pepper.

VIEL RISOTTO

Ingredients

rice 250-350 g
viel 700-800 g
dessert wine (prosek) 100 ml
dry white wine 100 ml
paprika powder 1 tsp
tomato paste 1 tbsp
beef bouillon cube
garlic 1-2 cloves
olive oil 4-5 tbsp
celery root 1
salt, pepper
onions 1-3
cloves 1-3
carrot 1
parsley

Preparation

Cut the meat into cubes. Peel and chop the onions. Grate the carrot and celery root. Chop the parsley. Crush the garlic.

Warm up the oil and fry the onions, carrot and celery, over low heat. After 5-10 minutes, add the meat. Fry the meat for a minute or two and then pour in the wine and add the paprika powder and the crushed meat bouillon cube.

Stew for a couple of minutes and then add the garlic, tomato paste and chopped parsley. Continue cooking for another half an hour. Then put in the rice and cook over medium heat, occasionally pouring in some water and stirring continuously, until the rice is cooked enough.

A few minutes before the risotto is done, add the dessert wine, salt and pepper. At the end, stir in olive oil (or a tablespoon of butter). Serve with grated cheese.

LAMB RISOTTO

Ingredients

rice 250-350 g
lamb meat 500-700 g
dried bacon (pancetta) 100 g
dry white wine 100 ml
lamb liver 50-70 g
olive oil 4-5 tbsp
garlic 1 clove
salt, pepper
onion 1

Preparation

Warm up the oil and fry the onions, over low heat. After 5-10 minutes, add the meat.

Fry the meat for a minute or two and then pour in the wine. Stew for a couple of minutes and then add the garlic. Continue cooking for another half an hour. Then put in the rice and cook over medium heat, occasionally pouring in some water and stirring continuously, until the rice is cooked enough.

A few minutes before the risotto is done, add the salt and pepper. At the end, stir in the olive oil (or a tablespoon of butter). Serve with grated cheese.

FISH
&
SEAFOOD

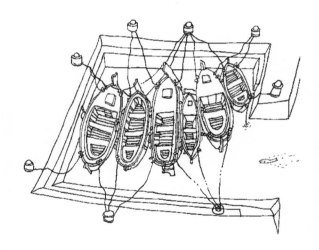

SARDINES IN LEMON JUICE

Ingredients

fresh sardines 1 kg / 2 lb
olive oil 5-6 tbsp
lemons 1-2
salt

Preparation

Clean and rinse the sardines. Transfer them into a pan. Do not pour any liquid (water or other), nor add any herbs or spices. Cover the pan and cook for 10-15 minutes, over moderate heat.

Drain the cooked anchovies and season them with a mixture of olive oil, lemon juice, salt and pepper.

Optional primary ingredients: mackerels instead of sardines.

SHAKEN CODFISH

Ingredients

dried codfish (stockfish)
400-500 g / 1 lb
(first-rate) olive oil 5-8 tbsp
potatoes 1 kg / 2 lb
garlic 3-4 cloves
(fresh) parsley
salt, pepper

Preparation

Soak the dried cod fish in water for 3-4 days, changing the water daily. Then cook the cod fish in fresh water. Clean the cooked fish and cut the meat into pieces.

Cook the (unpeeled) potatoes in water. After that, peel and cut them into slices, not too thin. Finely chop the parsley leaves and crush the peeled garlic cloves.

In a pot, alternately arrange layers of the sliced cooked potatoes and pieces of the cooked cod. Each potato layer as well as the cod layers season with oil, salt, pepper, parsley and garlic.

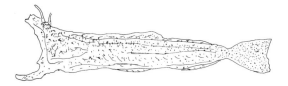

Cover the pan and hold it in a way that each fist holds a pot handle, but at the same time press the pot cover with your thumbs. Then energetically shake the covered pot, 10-15 times.

Optional primary ingredients: green olives, coarsley chopped.

CODFISH STEW

Ingredients

dried codfish (stockfish)
400-500 g / 1 lb
tomato paste 1-2 tsp
olive oil 5-8 tbsp
garlic 3-4 cloves
potatoes 2 lb
salt, pepper
parsley

Preparation

Soak the dried cod fish in water for 3-4 days, changing the water daily. Then cut the cod into pieces, removing the bones.

Peel the potatoes and cut them also into pieces, not too small.

Chop finely the parsley and garlic.

In a pot alternately arrange layers of cod and potatoe pieces. Each layer season with oil, salt, pepper, garlic and parsley. Add the tomato paste, but not much. Pour some water, not enough to exceed the level of the surface of the ingredients in the pot.

Cover the pot and cook over medium heat for 1-1.5 hours. Shake the pot from time to time, but do not stir the content.

Optional primary ingredients: bell peppers, leeks, broad beans, peas, mushrooms, pine nuts, raisins.

Optional herbs and spices: dry white wine, sweet wine, chili peppers, fried onions, black or green olives, carrots, milk, desalted anchovy fillets, basil, paprika powder, shallots, marjoram, vegetable bouillon powder, celery, capers, sour cherries, cloves, oregano, rosemary, bay leaves, apples, honey, cinnamon, nutmeg, lemon zest and juice, bread crumbs, vinegar, prunes, sugar.

COATED SARDINES

Ingredients

sardines 700 g / 1.5 lb.
bread crumbs 100-150 g
flour 50-80 g /1.5-3 oz
eggs 3-4
frying oil
salt

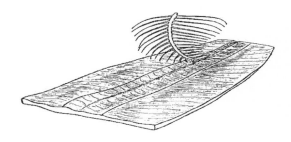

Preparation

Clean and rinse the sardines. Cut off the heads. Using a knife, open the sardines like a book and remove their spines (again using a knife, all along the spine).

Press the sardines in the flour, then dip them into the beaten eggs and finally press them in the bread crumbs to coat. Lay the fried breaded sardines on a paper towel to drain off. Salt and serve.

Optional herbs and spices to add to the beaten eggs: water, milk, vegetable bouillon powder or cube, grated cheese, crushed garlic, chopped parsley, chopped rocket salad, paprika powder, chili pepper, capers, olive oil (especially if the sardines are to be baked in a non-stick pan with no oil or butter, over low heat).

Optional herbs and spices to add to the bread crumbs: garlic, parsley, basil, lemon zest, rosemary, sage, chopped dried tomatoes.

Optional seasonings for the fried sardines: thin lemon slices or lemon juice, finely chopped parsley.

Suggestions: Cutting off the tail, before opening the sardine, facilitates the succeding process of opening the sardine and pulling off the spine.

Optional primary ingredients: peas, artichokes, tomatoes, potatoes, dried bacon, mushrooms, garbanzo beans (chickpeas), beans, lentils.

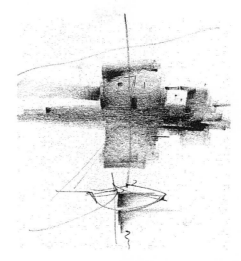

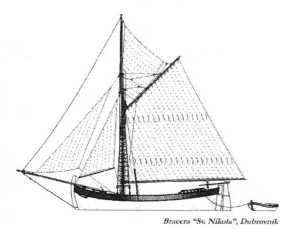

Bracera "Sv. Nikola", Dubrovnik

Optional herbs and spices: saffron, sweet wine, bay leaves, red wine, capers, basil, vegetable bouillon powder or cube, vinegar.

CUTTLEFISH WITH BROAD BEANS

Ingredients

cuttlefish 300 g
broad (fava) beans 500-700 g
dry white wine 100-150 ml
olive oil 4-5 tbsp
garlic 2-3 cloves
salt, pepper
onions 1-2
parsley

Preparation

Clean and rinse the cuttlefish. Cut the cuttlefish into pieces. Chop the garlic and parsley. In a pan warm up the oil. Fry the onions over low heat. Then add the garlic and parsley. Stir a couple of times and put in the cuttlefish and broad beans. Cook over medium heat for 20-30 minutes.

CUTTLEFISH SALAD

Ingredients

cuttlefish 1 kg / 2 lb
vinegar 100 ml / ½ cup
olive oil 4-5 tbsp
salt, pepper
onion 1-2

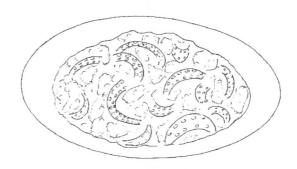

Preparation

Clean and rinse the cuttlefish. Cook the cuttlefish in water for 20-30 minutes. Cut the cooked cuttlefish into short sticks. Peel the onions and cut them into thin strips. After that, in a bowl mix the cuttlefish, onions, oil, vinegar, salt and pepper.

Optional ingredients: cooked potatoes, cheese, broad beens or chick peas, cooked or grilled squid, octopus, garlic, celery, parsley, basil, wild fennel, bay leaves, capers, tomatoes, black or green olives, rocket salad, pickled gherkins, chives, honey, shallots, lemon zest or juice.

Trajta, Korčula

Suggestions: The cuttlefish salad tastes the best when it is served a couple hours after the preparation.

FRIED SQUID

Ingredients

squid (calamari) 1,25 kg / 3 lb
frying oil
lemon 1
flour
salt

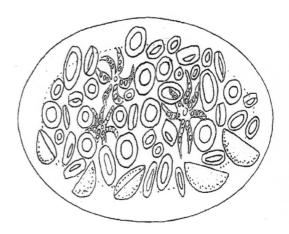

Preparation

Clean and rinse the squid. Drain the squid and then cut it into rings, not too narrow. Keep the squid in the refrigerator until needed.

Warm up an abundant quantity of the oil, over high heat. Take the squid out of the refrigerator and promptly proceed.

Press the squid rings in flour and fry them (not too many at one time) for a minute over high heat and later on over medium heat. Take them out as soon as they appear to be ready.

Salt the fried squid and serve immediately, with lemon segments or lemon juice and mayonnaise.

Optional herbs and spices for the

flour: garlic, parsley, paprika powder or cube, corn flour.

Optional seasonings for the fried squid: pepper, parsley, (white) vinegar, garlic, capers, oregano.

Suggestions: Change the frying oil after three batches.

STUFFED SQUID

Ingredients

squid (calamari) 800 g / 2 lb
bread crumbs 2-3 tbsp
olive oil 1-2 tbsp
rice 100 g / 3 oz
garlic 3-4 cloves
salt, pepper
parsley
flour

Preparation

Clean and rinse the squid. Chop finely the garlic and parsley. Cook the rice and drain it.

Fry briefly the squid heads and tentacles in some oil. Take them out and drain them. Then finely chop the heads and tentacles. Mix them in a bowl with the parsley, garlic, bread crumbs, rice, salt and pepper.

Use the mixture to fill in the squid mantles. Close the open ends of the mantles and fix them with toothpicks.

Press the stuffed squid mantles in

the flour. Fry them in some oil (not much).

Optional primary ingredients of the filling: scampi or shrimp tail meat, clam or mussel meat, cooked cuttlefish, fried mushrooms, pancetta (dried bacon), mortadella, ham, prosciutto ham, cooked egg yolks, beaten eggs, (raw o fried) fish meat, mashed cooked potatoes, canned tuna meat, cheese, ricotta cheese, fried zucchini, leeks, cooked peas, cooked broad beans, (dried) tomatoes, black or green olives, soft inside of a bread slice (soaked in milk or water and drained afterwards), figs, ground almonds, cooked barley, raisins (soaked and drained), (gently fried) pine nuts.

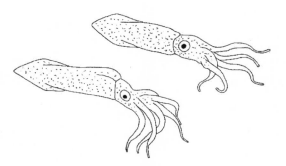

Optional herbs and spices for the filling: oregano, celery, lemon zest and juice, desalted anchovy fillets, tomato paste, basil, vegetable bouillon powder, rosemary, saffron, nutmeg, squid ink, cream, dry white wine, vinegar, sage, wild fennel, fried onions, green onions, capers, mint, chives.

Optional ingredients at the end: lemon juice, lemon slices, parsley, garlic, olive oil.

Possible omissions: rice, garlic.

Optional proceeding: Pour some wine (two or three tablespoons) two or three times during the frying process.

Different method: Bake the stuffed squid in an oven or grill them.

BAKED OCTOPUS

Ingredients

octopus, 2-3 smaller ones,
1.5-2 kg / 3-4 lb
potatoes 1-1.5 kg / 2-3 lb
olive oil 4-5 tbsp
salt, pepper

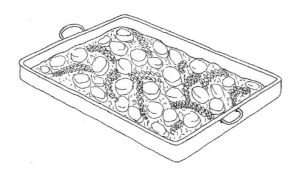

Preparation

Clean the octopuses, rinse them and cut them into pieces. Peel the potatoes and slice them.

In a baking pan lay the potatoes and over them arrange a layer of octopus cuts. Season with oil, salt and pepper. Then, if you want, you can stir everything up. Put the pan in a preheated oven and bake for app. an hour at a medium high temperature.

Optional primary ingredients: (red) bell peppers, zucchini, tomatoes, eggplants.

Optional herbs and spices: garlic, parsley, rosemary, dry white wine, (red) onions, green onions, bay leaves, carrots, shallots, green or black olives, lemon zest and juice, chili peppers, capers, sage, vegetable bouillon powder, paprika powder, apple, fresh figs, sweet wine.

Optional proceeding: Cover the baking pan.

Peka

Peka (baking under the bell) is a famous Dalmatian dish.

Ingredients (octopus, potatoes, oil and seasonings) are placed in a pan and subsequently covered with a bell-shaped lid and ambers on top,

After that follows the roasting.

eat and love Croatia

BUZARA

Ingredients

scampi 1 kg / 2 lb
or
clams or mussels 1.5-2 kg / 2 lb
dry white wine
100-200 ml / ½ - 1 cup
brandy (cognac, armagnac) 1-3 tbsp
bread crumbs 2-3 tbsp
tomato paste 1 tsp
olive oil 5-6 tbsp
garlic 2-4 cloves
salt, pepper
parsley

Preparation

Clean the clams, mussels or scampi. Chop finely the garlic and parsley.

In a large pan warm up the oil. Fry briefly the garlic and parsley, over low heat. Then stir in the crumbs.

Continue stirring for a minute or two and after that put in the clams, mussels or scampi. Stir for a minute. Pour in the wine and stir in the tomato paste. Let the wine partly evaporate. Continue cooking for another 10-15 minutes, pouring in some water, when needed. Minutes before removing the pan from the stove, season with salt, pepper and cognac.

Optional herbs and spices: lemon zest and juice, vegetable bouillon powder, chili pepper, paprika powder, celery, sweet wine, mint, sugar, green olives, oregano, saffron, bay leaves, pine nuts, ground almonds, shallots, onions, cream.

FISH PAPRIKASH

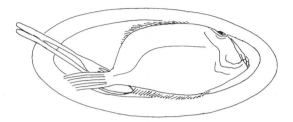

A fish stew (freshwater fish, white wine, onions, paprika, spices) traditionally cooked outdoors in a cauldron hanging over an open fire.

BAKED WRAPPED FISH

Ingredients

fish (whole or fillets) 1250 g
aluminum or parchment
or other type of roasting paper
selected herbs and spices
olive oil 4-5 tbsp
salt

Preparation

Clean and rinse the fish. Sprinkle the roasting paper with salt and spatter some olive oil. Place the fish on the roasting paper. Season the fish (inside and out) with selected herbs and spices. After that spatter some oil over the surface of the fish and then fold up the roasting paper.

Place the wrapped fish into a baking dish. Put it into a preheated oven and bake for 15-45 minutes (depending on the fish size) at a medium high temperature.

Optional ingredients: squid, cuttle-fish, scampi, shrimps, mussels or clams (shelled), grapes, black or green olives, tomatoes, potatoes, bell peppers, zucchini, eggplants, pickled gherkins, carrots, desalted anchovy fillets, rosemary, oregano, sage, basil, thyme, parsley, garlic, tomato paste or "passata", lemon zest or juice, dry white wine, butter, cognac (brandy), pepper, orange slices, lemon slices, bay leaves, onions, celery, cloves, wild fennel, marjoram, bread crumbs (previously fried in some oil), tomato sauce, capers.

Optional proceeding: Seasoned fish fillets may subsequently be rolled up, before being placed on the roasting paper.

Note: It is by no means obligatory to season the fish before wrapping and baking it. The fish may be seasoned after the baking (with salt, oil, parsley ...).

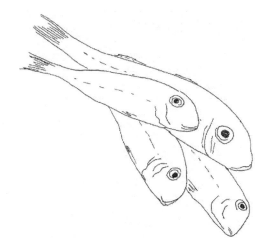

Optional herbs and spices: dry white wine, bread crumbs, fried onions, shallots, thyme, parsley.

RED MULLET FISH WITH ORANGE JUICE

Ingredients

red mullets 1 kg / 2 lb
olive oil 4-7 tbsp
oranges 1-2
salt, pepper

Preparation

Clean and rinse the fish, leaving the heads on.

In a wide pan pour 1-2 tablespoons of oil and then arrange layers of fish, every layer seasoned with salt and orange juice. Do not add water.

Cook for 15-20 minutes, over medium heat.

TUNA WITH LEMON SAUCE

Ingredients

fresh raw tuna 1 kg / 2 lb
olive oil 4-5 tbsp
bay leaves 3-4
salt, pepper
celery 1 rib
lemon 1-2
carrots 1
onion 1

Preparation

Cut the tuna meat into cubes, not too small.

Chop the celery and onion. Grate the carrot.

In a pan warm up the oil and fry the onions, celery and carrot, over low heat. After that, put in the tuna meat. Fry them over medium heat and then add the bay leaves and lemon juice. Season with salt and pepper.

Continue cooking on moderate heat, pouring some water from time to time. Do not stir, shake gently the pan. Black olives can be added.

CUTTLEFISH IN WINE

Ingredients

cuttlefish 1.25 kg / 2.5 – 3 lb
dry white wine 200 ml / 1 cup
tomato paste 1 tsp
olive oil 4-5 tbsp
salt, pepper
onions1-2

Preparation

Clean the cuttlefish, saving the ink bag (put it in a glass with some water). Rinse the cuttlefish and cut it into pieces, not too small. Peel the onions and chop it finely.

In a pan warm up the oil. Fry the onions over low heat. Then add the cuttlefish. Increase the heat to medium and stir for o minute or two. After that pour in the wine and let it almost evaporate. Stir in the potato paste and continue cooking, adding some water when needed. Season with salt and pepper. Minutes before removing the pan from the heat, stir in the ink, dissolved in water.

Optional herbs and spices: vegetable bouillon powder, garlic, parsley, bay leaves, lemon zest and juice.

TUNA SALAD

Mix in a bowl the canned tuna, salad tomatoes, basil, boiled vegetables (green beans, cauliflower, peas, carrots, corn), capers, celery, (white) onion, sugar, olive oil, salt, pepper.

Optional ingredients: yellow bell pepper, salted anchovies, boiled eggs, canned mushrooms, black or green olives, parsley, canned sardines.

ROASTED SQUID

Ingredients

squid 1 kg
olive oil 4-7 tbsp
garlic 1-3 cloves
salt, pepper
parsley

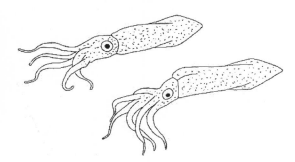

Preparation

Roast the squid, whole but cleaned, on a grill pan, without adding any oil.

Remove the roasted squid as soon as they are ready. Cut the roasted squid into pieces and season them with the crushed garlic, chopped parsley, salt, pepper and olive oil. Serve the squid immediately or later.

Optional ingredients: boiled potatoes.

Another method: Season the roasted squid with chopped (white) onions, olive oil, salt and pepper.

FISH BAKED IN FOIL

Ingredients

gilthead sea bream (orada), sea bass (lubin, branzin) or other kind of white fish 1-1.2 kg
olive oil 4-5 tbsp
garlic 1-2 cloves
parsley
salt

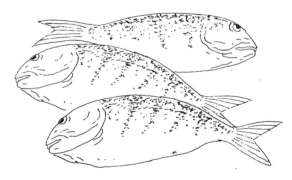

Preparation

Put the cleaned fish on a sheet of aluminium foil. Fold the foil 2-3 times. Bake the fish on a grill pan or in the oven. Cook for 20-30 minutes over medium heat.

Season the baked fish with the olive oil, crushed garlic, chopped parsley, salt and pepper.

Before closing the foil, you can add potatoes, carrots, garlic, tomatoes, zucchini, dill or onions.

SARDINES AND POTATOES

Ingredients

sardines 3-4 cans
potatoes 60-75 dag
garlic 1-3 cloves
salt, pepper
parsley

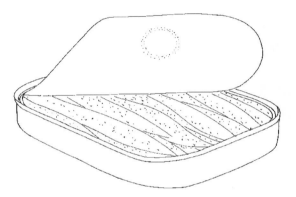

Preparation

Cook the potatoes in boiling water, without peeling them first. Peel the boiled potatoes and then cut them to pieces or crush them.

Cut the sardines into pieces, large or small. Crush the garlic. Mince the parsley leaves.

In a bowl, mix the sardines, potatoes, garlic, parsley, oil, salt and paper.

Optional ingredients: boiled carrots or peas, boiled eggs, pickled gherkins, ham, maionnaise, lemon juice and zest, onions, capers, bell peppers, salted anchovies, tomatoes, canned tuna fish, vinegar, mustard.

eat and love Croatia

OYSTERS

The most renowned varieties come from Ston on Pelješac in Dalmatia, and the Limski kanal in Istria.

Oysters are delicious raw, although they are tasty even in risottos, soup, as well as grilled or braised.

Raw oysters

Rinse the fresh oysters under tap water. Open them with a suitable knife (covering the hand in which you hold the shell with a piece of cloth).

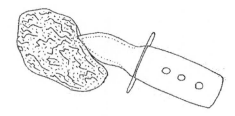

Separate and eliminate the intenstines from the oyster meat. Remember to loosen the oyster meat from its shell so that slurping is made easy. Preserve the sea water inside.

Season every shell with a few drops of lemon juice and serve the oysters.

Grilled oysters

Rinse the fresh oysters under tap water, open them with a suitable knife (covering the other hand with a piece of cloth). Separate and eliminate the intenstines from the oyster meat. Remember to loosen the oyster meat from its shell in order to enable easy eating.

Discard the flat shell covers, the empty part of the shell.

Chop the garlic and parsley. Mix them with some olive oil, bread crumbs, salt and pepper. Add dry white wine and lemon juice (maybe zest as well).

Pour some oil (or melted butter) in all the preserved shells. Then also disperse the garlic and parsley mix.

Grill the prepared shells for 5-6 minutes.

Serve the oysters but let them cool down for a few minutes before consumption.

FRIED SHRIMP

Ingredients

shrimp (small) 700-800 g
frying oil
flour
salt

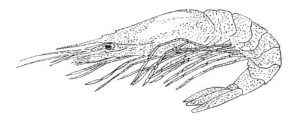

Preparation

Very fresh small shrimp, with or without its shell, roll in flour, lighty.

Warm up a lot of frying oil and fry the shrimp in hot deep oil.

Do not crowd the shrimp while frying.

Drain the fried shrimp and season them with salt.

Optional ingredients: fried smelt fish, fried squid, fried cuttlefish.

Optional herbs and spices for the fried prawns: garlic, parsley, lemon juice.

OCTOPUS WITH POTATOES

Ingredients

(frozen) octopus 1-1,2 kg
potatoes 500-700 g
olive oil 5-6 tbsp
garlic 1-3 cloves
salt, pepper
parsley

Preparation

Cook the octopus (put it frozen in the water) and the potatoes, separately.

In a bowl, mix the boiled octopus and potatoes, both cut to pieces. Season with the olive oil, garlic, parsey, salt and pepper.

Optional ingredients: vegetable bouillon powder, paprika powder.

CAPESANTE

Known as the pilgrim scallop or Saint-Jacques Shell, this Istrian shellfish is considered to be one of the tastiest.

The scallop is usually accompanied by the superb Istrian olive oil.

eat and love Croatia

BRODET
(fish stew)

Ingredients

white fish (conger, scorpion fish
or/and other) 1-1.5 kg
fresh tomatoes 100-500 g
or
tomato paste 1-5 tbsp
white wine 70-100 ml
olive oil 5-6 tbsp
garlic 1-3 cloves
salt, pepper
onion 1-3
parsley

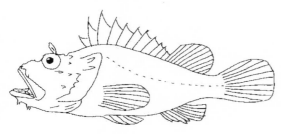

Preparation

Clean the fish and cut it in large pieces.

Peel the tomatoes and cut them to pieces. Chop the onions, garlic and parsley.

In a wide pot warm up the oil. Fry the onions over low heat. After a few minutes put in the fish and season with garlic, parsley, dry white wine, tomatoes, salt and pepper. Pour in some water, just barely enough to cover the fish, no more than that.

Cook until the fish begins (only begins!) to fall apart, over low heat.

Suggestion: During the cooking process, do not stir the pot, just shake it. It is better not to put the lid on the pot.

Optional proceeding: Clean the fish so thoroughly that no bones remain in the fish meat. That proceed with the cooking process, but adding also potatoes, cut to large pieces.

Note: Instead of the white fish, mackerel or sardines can be used.

Another suggestion: The brodet is usually served with polenta, a traditional dish prepared of ground corn.

EEL AND FROG BRODET
(NERETVA VALLEY BRODET)

This is a special kind of fish stew, so called "Neretvanski brodet", prepared by using eel fish cuts and frog parts, adding to the original ingredients of a brodet also the vinegar, hot bell peppers or chili peppers and bay leaves.

MARINATED TUNA

Ingredients

tuna fish 1 kg
black olives 12-15
vinegar 3-5 tbsp
garlic 1-2 cloves
olive oil 100 ml
bay leaves 2-5
salt, pepper
sugar 1 tsp
onions 1-2
rosemary
lemon 1
parsley
flour

Preparation

Cut the tuna meat in slices and roll them slightly in flour. Chop the onions, garlic and parsley.

Fry the tuna slices in olive oil, over medium heat. Remove the fried slices and transfer them to a bowl.

Use the same oil to gently fry the onions. After a couple of minutes add the garlic and parsley. Stir a few times and then add the rosemary, bay leaves, sugar, salt and pepper. Pour in the vinegar and let the marinade cook over low heat for 2-3 minutes. After that pour the marinade over the fried fish. Cool down the marinated fish and put it into the refrigerator.

Serve the marinated tuna slices with the marinade and black olives, chopped parsley and lemon slices.

Note: Sardines can be marinated the same way.

SHRIMP IN HONEY

Ingredients

shrimp (small) 250-300 g
olive oil 4-5 tbsp
garlic 1-2 cloves
honey 1-2 tbsp
flour

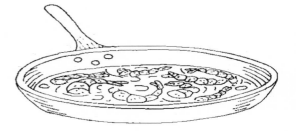

Preparation

Very fresh small shrimp, with or without its shell, roll in flour, lighty.

Warm up the olive oil and fry the shrimp, with chopped garlic. Stir in the honey and continue cooking over low heat a couple more minutes. Then pour in some dry white wine, not much. When the wine evaporates, stir in chopped parsley. Serve immediately.

Optional ingredients: brandy, rosemary, lemon juice (at the end), thyme, pepper.

VEGETABLES

STUFFED ARTICHOKES

Ingredients

artichokes 8-12
ingredients of the selected filling
ripe tomatoes 100-400 g
olive oil 4-5 tbsp
sale, pepe
onion 1

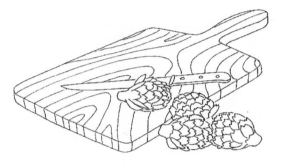

Preparation

Wash the artichokes, drain them off and proceed with the trimming. Cut off the top of the artichokes, using a knife. Eliminate the outer leaves which are too "woody". Cut off also the sharp points from some of the remaining leaves, this time using kitchen scissors. Then place the artichokes in water with lemon juice in it. Let them soak for 10-15 minutes. After doing that, drain them off well. Then open the artichoke leaves, pushing them outside.

Stuff the "blossomed" artichokes with the selected filling.

Peel the tomatoes and cut them into pieces. Chop the onions.

In a wide pan warm up the oil. Fry the onions over low heat. Then add the tomatoes. Lay the stuffed artichokes in the pan, spatter some oil and pour some water.

Cover the pan and cook over low or moderate heat for 20-30 minutes.

Garlic and parsley filling: Prepare a mixture of finely chopped parsley, garlic, bread crumbs, salt and pepper.

Meat filling: Prepare a mixture of ground meat, bread crumbs, egg(s), grated cheese, parsley, salt and pepper.

Tuna fish filling: Prepare a mixture of canned tuna, desalted anchovy fillets, capers, garlic, parsley, salt and pepper.

Desalted anchovy filling: Prepare a mixture of desalted anchovy fillets, bread crumbs, garlic, marjoram, parsley, raisins, olive oil, pine nuts and grated cheese.

Caper filling: Prepare a mixture of desalted capers, bread crumbs (slightly toasted in some oil), desalted anchovy fillets, garlic and parsley.

Optional ingredients of the filling: marjoram, pancetta (dried bacon), ham, prosciutto ham, mortadella, grated cheese, soft inside of a bread slice, soaked in milk and then squeezed out, scampi or shrimp tail meat, eggs, cooked egg yolks, whole cooked eggs, ground meat, thyme, wild fennel, vegetable bouillon powder or cube, mint, paprika powder, rosemary, orange juice, dry white wine, bay leaves, capers.

Optional herbs and spices of the sauce: dry white wine, vegetable bouillon powder, balsamic vinegar (aceto balsamico), paprika powder, grated cheese, desalted anchovy fillets.

Optional proceeding: Put broad beans, peas, potatoes, meat (cut or ground), squid or cuttlefish (cut into pieces) amongst the artichokes, before the beginning of the cooking.

STUFFED BELL PEPPERS

Ingredients

green bell peppers (or red or yellow)
8 pieces
ripe tomatoes 35o-600 g / 12-25 oz
bread crumbs 1-2 tsp
olive oil 4-5 tbsp
salt, peppers

meat filling:

ground (baby) beef meat 400-500 g
/ 13-17 oz
ground pork meat 250-400 g / 10-13
oz
vegetabe bouillon powder
garlic 2-4 cloves
salt, pepper
onions 1-2
eggs 1-2
parsley

Preparation

Cut off the top of the bell peppers and remove the seeds from the inside. Then wash them and let them drain off.

Chop the onions, garlic and parsley. Peel the tomatoes and cut them into pieces.

In a pan warm up the oil. Fry the onions over low heat. Put in the meat and stir a couple of times. Let the meat fry over medium heat, until the liquid almost evaporates. Then remove the pan from the heat and let the meat cool down.

Stir the eggs, garlic and parsley into the meat and then also the vegetable bouillon powder or a cube, salt and pepper.

Stuff the peppers with the prepared meat filling.

Arrange the stuffed peppers in a wide pot. Add the tomatoes and pour some water, enough to reach to the 4/5 of the level of the peppers. Season with salt and pepper. Cover the pot and cook over moderate heat. Agitate the pot every now and then. Minutes before removing the pot from the heat, add some bread crumbs, but not much.

Optional ingredients of the filling: other types of meat, rice, pancetta (dried bacon), mashed cooked potatoes, grated raw potatoes, cooked eggs, bread crumbs, mushrooms,

eat and love Croatia

black or green olives, pasta cooked very much "al dente", cheese, ricotta cheese, grated cheese, fresh cheese, cream, sour cream, paprika powder, soft inside of eggplants or zucchini, tomato paste, basil, capers, nutmeg, wild fennel, chili peppers, celery, rosemary, oregano, chives, carrots, mint, desalted anchovy fillets, pine nuts, soft inside of a bread slice, soaked in water or milk, and then squeezed out, canned tuna fish instead of meat, raisins.

Optional herbs and spices for the sauce: bay leaves, garlic, vegetable buillon powder, grated carrots, parsley, celery, vinegar.

Optional ingredients at the end: cream, sour cream, grated cheese.

Possible omissions: beef meat.

Different method: Bake the stuffed peppers in an oven.

PEA STEW

Ingredients

peas (fresh or frozen)
700 g / 1½ lb
pancetta (dried bacon)
100-200 g / 3-7 oz
tomato paste 1 tsp
olive oil 4-5 tbsp
garlic 2-3 tbsp
salt, pepper
onions 1-2
parsley

Preparation

Cut the pancetta (dried bacon) into small cubes. Finely chop the onions, garlic and parsley.

Warm up the oil in a pan. Fry the pancetta, onions, garlic and parsley,

over low heat, stirring often. After a few minutes, add the peas and stir in the tomato paste. Cook for another 15-20 minutes over medium heat. Season with salt and pepper.

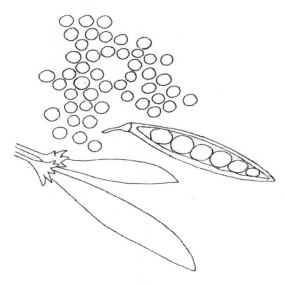

Optional ingredients: potatoes, (ground) meat, mushrooms, broad beans, chickpeas (already cooked).

Optional herbs and spices: vegetable bouillon powder, carrot, thyme, bay leaves, mint, basil, nutmeg, sugar, cloves, capers, dry white wine, red wine, saffron, cream, grated cheese.

COATED ZUCCHINI

Ingredients

zucchini 600 g / 20 oz
bread crumbs
salt, pepper
eggs 2-3
frying oil
flour

Preparation

Cut the zucchini into slices, not too

thin. Press the zucchini slices in the flour, then in the beaten eggs and finally in the crumbs to coat.

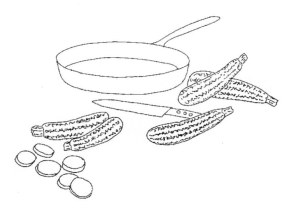

Fry the coated zucchini slices in an abundant quantity of oil. The fried slices put on kitchen paper towels to drain off.

Optional herbs and spices for the beaten eggs: vegetable buillon powder, grated cheese, cream, milk.

TOMATO AND CHEESE SALAD

Ingredients

salad tomatoes 500 g / 1 lb
cheese (mozzarella or feta)
250 g / 10 oz
olive oil 3-4 tbsp
garlic 1 clove
salt, pepper
basil

Preparation

Clean, rinse and cut the tomatoes. Drain the mozzarella and cut it into cubes. Chop the garlic and basil.

In a salad bowl mix the tomatoes, mozzarella, garlic, basil, salt, pepper and olive oil.

Leave the salad to rest for 15-20 minutes and then serve it.

Optional herbs and spices: oregano instead of basil.

VEGETABLE STEW

Ingredients

yellow bell pepper 1
ripe tomatoes 2-5
red bell pepper 1
olive oil 4-5 tbsp
celery 1-3 ribs
eggplants 1-2
potatoes 1-2
salt, pepper
onions 1-2
basil

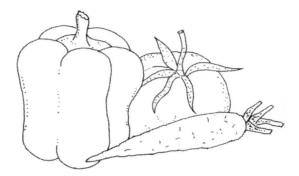

Preparation

Clean and rinse the eggplants. Without peeling them, cut the eggplants into small cubes. Sprinkle them with some salt and allow the eggplants to rest salted for half an hour, or an hour, to loose the bitter juices. Then rinse the eggplants and drain them off.

Clean the bell peppers and cut them into pieces. Peel the tomatoes and cut them too. Peel the potatoes and slice them. Chop finely the onions, basil and celery.

eat and love Croatia

In a pan warm up the oil. Fry the onions over low heat. After that, add all the other vegetables. Cook for 5-6 minutes over medium heat, stirring often. Then season with salt and pepper and pour in the water, as much as is needed to barely cover the ingredients.

Continue cooking for 30-45 minutes over moderate heat. Stir every now and then, pouring in some water, not much, when needed.

Optional primary ingredients: zucchini, black or green olives.

Optional herbs and spices: vegetable bouillon powder, garlic, oregano, capers, parsley, sugar, vinegar.

Optional ingredients at the end: eggs.

POTATOES WITH ONIONS

Ingredients

potatoes 850 g / 2 lb
olive oil 4-5 tbsp
salt, pepper
onions 1-2
parsley

Preparation

Peel the potatoes and cut them into pieces.

In a pan warm up the oil. Fry the finely chopped onions, over low heat. Then add the potatoes. Cook over medium heat, stirring often. When necessary, pour in some water.

Minutes before removing the pan off the heat, season with finely chopped parsley, salt and pepper.

BOILED CHICKPEAS

Ingredients

chickpeas 500 g / 1 lb
olive oil 6-7 tbsp
salt, pepper

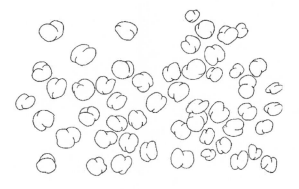

Preparation

Let the chickpeas soak in (warm) water for 12-24 hours.

Cook the chickpeas in water with some oil and salt, over moderate heat. At the end, season with pepper. Add some more salt and oil, if needed.

Optional primary ingredients: potatoes, barley, pancetta (dried bacon), leeks, canned tuna, sausages.

Optional herbs and spices: sage, rosemary, celery, bay leaves, garlic, onions, vegetable bouillon powder or cube, parsley, thyme, paprika powder, chili peppers, tomato paste, lemon zest and juice, vinegar.

COATED MUSHROOMS

Ingredients

white button mushrooms
(champignon) 500 g / 1 lb
bread crumbs
frying oil
eggs 3
flour
salt

Preparation

Clean the mushrooms and separate the caps from the stalks. Press them in the flour, then in the beaten eggs and then in the crumbs to coat.

Fry the coated mushrooms in an abundant quantity of frying oil,

over medium heat. Remove the fried mushrooms from the oil and put them on paper towels to drain off.

Optional herbs and spices for the beaten eggs: vegetable bouillon powder, grated cheese, parsley, oregano, thyme, basil, cream.

Optional ingredients at the end: mayonnaise, lemon juice.

VARA

Vara is one of the traditional dishes of the region of Dubrovnik.

Pour 3-4 glasses of water in a big pot. Add broad beans, peas, beans, chickpeas, lentils and other kinds of dry legumes, all previously soaked in water (overnight), as well as various kinds of cereals, such as wheat, barley or rye, with olive oil and tomatoes or tomato paste. Vegetable bouillon powder is optional. Cook for hours, until all the ingredients soften enough.

eat and love Croatia

BELL PEPPER STEW

Preparation

Seed the bell peppers and cut them into short and narrow sticks. Peel the tomatoes and cut them into pieces. Chop the onions and the garlic.

In a pan warm up the oil. Fry the onions over low heat. Soon add the garlic. Then put in the bell peppers and continue cooking for 5-6 minutes, over medium heat. After that add the tomatoes. Cook for half an hour, still over medium heat. Stir from time to time, pouring in some water when necessary. Minutes before the end of the cooking, season the dish with the parsley and salt.

Optional ingredients: eggplants, zucchini, potatoes, olives, rice, sausages, pancetta (dried bacon), basil, oregano, bay leaves, vinegar, dry white wine, marjoram, thyme, mint, capers, desalted anchovy fillets.

Optional ingredients at the end: grated cheese, paprika, vinegar.

BOILED CAULIFLOWER

Ingredients

cauliflower 1 kg / 1 lb
olive oil 2-3 tbsp
grated cheese
bread crumbs
oregano
salt

Preparation

In a pan warm the oil and add the bread crumbs and oregano. Stir a couple of minutes and then remove the pan from the heat. Minutes later stir in the grated cheese also.

Cook the cauliflower in water. Drain it, divide it into small parts and season them with the prepared mixture of olive oil, fried crumbs, oregano and cheese.

GNOCCHI WITH CHEESE

Ingredients

potato gnocchi 1 kg / 2 lb
mozzarella 200-300 g / 7-10 oz
grated cheese 100 g / 3 oz
ripe tomatoes 1 kg / 2 lb
olive oil 3-4 tbsp
salt, pepper
onions 2
sugar
basil

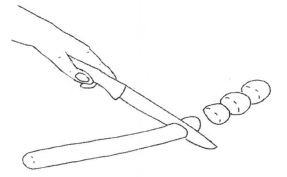

Preparation

Using the tomatoes, onions, basil, olive oil, salt, and a pinch of sugar, prepare the tomato sauce.

Drain the mozzarella and cut it into little cubes.

Cook the gnocchi in boiling salted water. Drain them and lay them into a baking pan. Pour over the sauce and put the mozzarella cubes. Sprinkle with grated cheese.

Preheat the oven at a high temperature. Let the gnocchi bake, but only for a minute or two.

Optional herbs and spices: garlic instead or beside the onions.

PEASENT STYLE POTATOES

Ingredients

potatoes 1 kg / 2 lb
olive oil 5-6 tbsp
salt, pepper
rosemary
sage

Preparation

Peel and rinse the potatoes. Cut them into pieces, not too small.

Warm the oil in a pan. Put in the potatoes, rosemary and sage. Season

with salt and pepper. Cook over medium heat, stirring very often.

Optional herbs and spices: vegetable bouillon powder, tomato paste, onions, garlic, parsley.

EGGPLANTS AU GRATIN

Ingredients

eggplants 1 kg / 2 lb
mozzarella cheese 200 g / 7 oz
grated cheese 100 g / 3 oz
tomatoes 1 kg / 1 lb
olive oil 5-6 tbsp
onion 1 (small)
garlic 2 cloves
parsley
salt

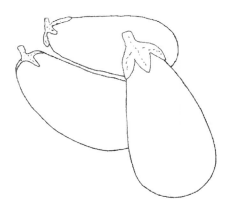

Preparation

With the tomatoes and oil prepare a tomato sauce. Remove the sauce from the heat and stir in the chopped parsley and salt.

Peel the eggplants and cut them into slices, not too thin. Sprinkle them with salt and let them rest for half an hour, to let them release the bitter juices. Then rinse and drain them off.

eat and love Croatia

Press the eggplant slices into flour and then fry them in some oil. Put the fried eggplant slices on kitchen paper towels to drain them off.

Pour one half of the tomato sauce into a baking oven. Then lay the eggplant slices in the sauce and cover them with the remaining tomato sauce. Sprinkle with grated cheese and lay over the mozzarella cheese slices.

Repeat the procedure until all the ingredients are exhausted.

Bake the seasoned eggplants for 30-40 minutes at a moderate temperature.

Optional ingredients: zucchini slices, cooked eggs, boiled potatoes, basil.

Optional proceeding: Grill the eggplant slices instead of frying them.

BOILED CHARD

Ingredients

chard 400-600 g
potatoes 150-250 g
olive oil 4-5 tbsp
salt, pepper

Preparation

Cook the chard and the potatoes, cut into pieces, in boiling water.

Drain the chard and the potatoes. Crush them, but not too much, while they are still in the pot.

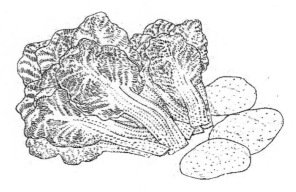

Season with the olive oil, salt and pepper. Let the chard simmer for minute or two, over medium heat.

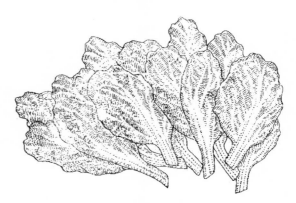

Optional ingredients: vegetable bouillon powder, garlic, vinegar.

BEANS

Ingredients

dry beans 400-600 g
or
fresh or frozen fresh beans
500-800 g
olive oil 4-7 tbsp

bay leaves 2-5
salt, pepper

BRAISED PEAS

Ingredients

fresh or frozen peas 500-800 g
dried bacon 100-200 g
tomato paste 1 tsp
olive oil 4-5 tbsp
garlic 2-3 cloves
salt, pepper
onions 1-2
parsley

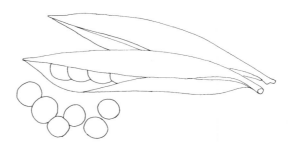

Preparation

Cook the beans in boiling water, with the bay leaves, until they soften quite well.

Drain the boiled beans. Season them with the olive oil, salt and pepper.

Optional ingredients: dried bacon, sa-usages, corn, (red) lentils, carrots, soup pasta.

Optional herbs and spices: thyme, vegetable bouillon powder, roux, garlic, tomato paste, paprika, parsley, (green) onions, tomato sauce.

Preparation

Fry the diced bacon and the chopped onions, crushed garlic and minced parsley, in the olive oil, over low heat. Stir all the time. After a minute or two add the peas. Stir in the tomato paste, but not much. Salt and pepper.

Keep stirring over medium heat, for a minute and then let the peas continue cooking, stirring occasionally, pouring in some water, also from time to time.

Optional ingredients: rice, meat, potatoes, mushrooms, broad beans.

Optional herbs and spices: vegetable bouillon powder or cube, celery, carrots, thyme, bay leaves, fennel, basil, nutmeg, sugar, capers, rosemary, cooking cream, dill, red or dry white wine, bread crumbs, grated cheese.

ROASTED MASHED POTATOES

Ingredients

potatoes 1 kg
olive oil 4-5 tbsp
onions 2-4
salt

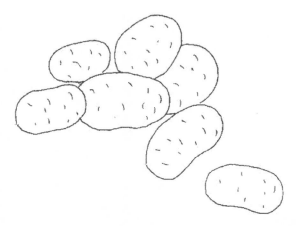

Preparation

Cook the potatoes in boiling water, without peeling them first.

In the meantime, peel and finely chop the onions. Let them fry in olive oil, in a large pan, over low heat, as long as it takes the onions to almost caramelize. Add a pinch of salt.

Peel the boiled potatoes, cut them to pieces and then crush them with a fork.

Add the mashed potatoes to the caramelised onions and raise the heat to medium. Stir for a couple of times.

Optional ingredients when frying the onions - dried bacon, leeks, bell peppers, and for the seasoned potatoes - vegetable bouillon powder, pepper, paprika, nutmeg, rosemary, tomato paste, cooking cream, sour cream, parsley, garlic, lemon juice or zest, egg yolk or vinegar.

POTATO AND TUNA SALAD

Ingredients

potatoes 1 kg
salad tomatoes 150-200 g
lemon juice 1-3 tbsp
salted anchovies 2-5
black olives 10-12
tuna fish 1-2 cans
olive oil 4-5 tbsp
vinegar 1-2 tbsp
salt, pepper
onions 1-2
eggs 1-2

Preparation

Cook the potatoes in boiling water, without peeling them first.

Coarsley crush the canned tuna fish.

Clean the tomatoes and slice them.

Boil the eggs and cut them to pieces.

Cut the salted anchovies to small pieces.

Peel the boiled potatoes and then cut them into slices.

In a bowl, mix very carefully the potatoes and all other ingredients. Stir in, if found necessary, some water, but not too much. Serve immediately.

Optional ingredients: boiled green beans or zucchini, green olives, canned sardines.

Lemon juice can be omitted.

BRAISED POTATOES

Ingredients

potatoes 1 kg
tomatoes 300-500 g
olive oil 4-5 tbsp
garlic 2-3 cloves
salt, pepper
parsley

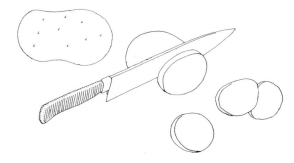

Preparation

In a pot warm up the oil. Add the minced parsley leaves and crushed garlic. Stir a couple of times, over low heat. Then put in the sliced potatoes and the tomatoes, cut to small pieces. Pour in half a glass of water. Season with salt and pepper. Cook over medium heat for a few minutes and then lower the heat. Continue cooking until the potatoes soften enough. While cooking, do not stir the content of the pot. Shake it.

Optional ingredients: onions, green onions, dried bacon, boiled green beans, leeks, ground meat, bell peppers, peas, celery, mushrooms, vegetable bouillon powder or cube, green olives, nutmeg, carrots, dry white wine, vinegar, fennel, rosemary, oregano, thyme, basil, sage, marjoram, paprika, grated cheese.

BOILED BRUSSELS SPROUTS

Ingredients

Brussels sprouts 600-800 g
olive oil 4-5 tbsp
salt, pepper

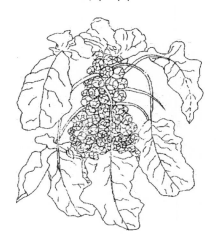

Preparation

Cook the Brussels sprouts in boiling water. Peeled potatoes can be added.

Drain the boiled sprouts and season them with the olive oil, salt and pepper.

Optional ingredients: vinegar, crushed garlic, vegetable bouillon powder, separately boiled dried bacon or sausages,

Different method: Braise the sprouts with potatoes, in olive oil.

___

RUSHTAN

Ingredients

rushtan (rushtika, collard greens, Dalmatian kale) 1 kg
vegetable bouillon powder 1 tsp
potatoes 150-250 g
olive oil 4-5 tbsp
salt, pepper

Preparation

Cook the Dalmatian kale (rushtika, Brassica oleracea var. Acephala), sliced very thinly, with peeled potatoes, in boiling water.

Drain the kale and the potatoes, already cooked and softened enough. Crush them using the appropriate kitchen tool. Season with olive oil, bouillon powder, salt and pepper.

Optional ingredients: dried bacon, boiled separately, garlic, tomato paste.

___

MIXED SALAD

Ingredients

lettuce 200-300 g
apple cider vinegar 1-2 tbsp
arugula 50-150 g
olive oil 4-5 tbsp
salt, pepper
carrot 1
apple 1

Preparation

Mix in a bowl the salad, arugula, grated apple, grated carrot, olive oil, vinegar, salt and pepper.

Optional ingredients: white cabbage, tomatoes, sage, parsley, celery.

___

BOILED
BROAD BEANS

Ingredients

fresh or frozen broad beans 1 kg
olive oil 4-5 tbsp
salt, pepper

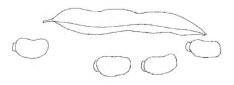

Preparation

Cook the broad beans in boiling water. The boiled broad beans season with oil, salt and pepper.

Optional ingredients: vinegar, vegetable bouillon powder, mozzarella, feta cheese.

STUFFED EGGPLANTS

Ingredients

middle-sized eggplants 4
fresh tomatoes 50-80 g
grated cheese 3-5 tbsp
tomato paste 1-2 tbsp
olive oil 4-5 tbsp
garlic 1-2 cloves
bread crumbs
salt, pepper
onions 2-3
parsley

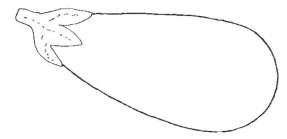

Stuffed eggplants can be cooked by stewing, frying or baking.

Preparation

Clean the eggplants and cut each one in half, longitudinally. Cut out the soft part, not too deeply. Sprinkle with salt. After half an hour, rinse the eggplants under tap water and let then dry off. Then cut the eggplant "meat" in pieces.

Chop the onions, garlic and parsley. Peel the tomatoes and mince them.

Gently fry the eggplant "meat" and the onions on a few tablespoons of olive oil, in a large frying pan. Remove them soon. Leave, in some of the oil, some of the fried onions. Mix the fried eggplants and part of the fried onions, in a bowl, with the garlic, parsley, tomato paste, grated cheese, breadcrumbs, salt and pepper. With this filling, stuff the eggplant "shells" preserved earlier.

Lay down the stuffed eggplants in the frying pan. Put in the minced tomatoes. Cover the lid and cook for an hour or so, over low heat. Optional ingredients: eggs, paprika, vegetable bouillon powder.

Meat filling

Dried bacon (pancetta), bread crumbs, ground meat, minced eggplant "meat", grated cheese, eggs, garlic, parsley, salt, pepper.

Optional ingredients: fried onions, paprika, vegetable bouillon powder, basil, dry white wine, fresh cheese, minced mushrooms, boiled rice, chili peppers, capers, thyme, cinnamon, nutmeg, black or green olives.

Cheese filling: minced cheese, black olives, capers, tomatoes, salt, grated cheese, ham.

KALAMPAJSANI KALAMPER

Ingredients

potatoes 1 kg
lard, oil or butter 1-3 tbsp
paprika powder
onions 2-3
salt

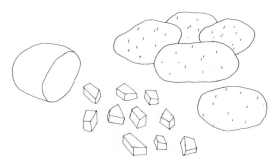

Preparation

Peel the potatoes and cut them into pieces.

Peel and finely chop the onions. Let them fry in olive oil, in a large pan, over low heat, as long as it takes the onions to almost caramelize. Season with a pinch of salt. Then add the potatoes and stew until the potatoes are cooked enough. From time to time pour in some water and stir. A few minutes before the dish is done stir in the paprika powder and salt.

Optional ingredients: sausages, smoked bacon, vegetable bouillon powder, garlic, parsley, pepper.

Note: This is a traditional dish popular in the region of Medjimurje.

TRUFFLES

Istria's Motovun forests contain some of the highest concentrations of truffles (Croatian - tartufi) in the world. Traditionally, truffles are served on pasta, risotto, fried eggs or meat.

In the spring, white truffles can be found in the woods, in the summer both white and black, and in the winter the black truffles are dominant.

BAKED ZUCCHINI WITH CHEESE

Ingredients

3-5 zucchini
olive oil or butter 1-3 tbsp
grated cheese 70-120 g
salt, pepper

Preparation

Cut the zucchini into quarters, or halve them if they are thin, lengthwise. Line them up in a single layer, in a baking dish already drizzled with olive oil, sprinkle them with more olive oil, season with salt and pepper, and then cover them with a layer of grated cheese.

Put the zucchini into the preheated oven and bake for 15-25 minutes, until they get the golden brown crust, but still remain tender. Serve immediately, possibly sprinkled with lemon zest or minced parsley.

Optional ingredients: mozzarella, breadcrumbs, onions, basil, thyme, garlic, vegetable bouillon powder or the egg, milk and sour cream mix.

BAKED BEANS

Ingredients

boiled or canned beans 500 g
diced and fried dry bacon 100-150 g
chopped and fried onion 1
olive oil or butter 1-3 tbsp
minced garlic 1-2 cloves
tomato paste 1-2 tbsp
salt, pepper

Preparation

Season the (almost fully) boiled beans with all the specified ingredients.

Pour the beans into a baking pan, cover it with a foil, and then bake for one hour. After that, uncover the pan and bake for ten minutes more.

Optional ingredients: bell peppers, sugar, paprika, Tabasco or Worcestershire sauce, vegetable bouillon powder, parsley, celery, roux (gently fried flour in olive oil), peperoncino.

ZUCCHINI FRITTERS

Ingredients

grated zucchini 3-4
beaten eggs 2-3
baking powder
salt, pepper
lemon zest
frying oil
parsley
flour

Preparation

In a bowl, mix all the ingredients. The final consistency of the mix should be such that you need a spoon to transfer the fritters to the pan.

Fry the fritters, not too many each time, in deep hot oil.

Optional ingredients: diced and fried dry bacon, chopped and fried onion, vegetable bouillon powder, paprika, parsley, peperoncino.

LEEKS WITH MUSHROOMS

Ingredients

sliced leeks 200-300 g
sliced porcini mushrooms 200-300 g
pumpkin seed oil 100 ml
salt, pepper

Preparation

Gently fry the leeks and porcini mushrooms with pumpkin seed oil. Season with salt and pepper.

MEAT

BRAISED MEAT ROLLS

Ingredients

pork, beef or veal slices 1 kg / 2 lb
pancetta (dried bacon)
100 g-150 g / 3-4 oz
tomato paste 1-2 tsp
olive oil 4-5 tbsp
garlic 1-3 cloves
dry white wine
100 ml / ½ cup
salt, pepper
cloves 1-3
nutmeg
parsley
flour

Preparation

In a bowl mix the chopped dry bacon, garlic and parsley, grated nutmeg, salt and pepper.

Spread a thin layer of the prepared mixture over each meat slice (previously beaten if necessary). Roll tightly the meat slices and fasten them with toothpicks. Press the meat rolls in flour and fry them in oil for a minute or two, over medium heat.

Pour in the wine and let it almost evaporate, still over medium heat. After that, add the tomato paste (or diced fresh tomatoes), pour in some water and put in the cloves.

Cover the pot and continue cooking for another 30-45 minutes.

A moment before turning off, add a tablespoon of parsley.

Optional ingredients of the filling: sausages, mortadella, breadcrumbs, chicken livers, grated cheese, ham, ground meat, beaten eggs, oregano, mozzarella or other type of cheese.

Optional herbs and spices for the sauce: rosemary, vegetable bouillon powder, dill, celery, carrot, onions, basil, bay leaves, raisins, sage, cooking cream.

Possible omissions: tomato paste.

BACON WRAPPED MEAT ROLLS

Ingredients

pork, beef or veal slices 1 kg / 2 lb
dry white wine 100 ml / ½ cup
dalmatian seasoning mix 1 tsp
sliced ham 100-120 g / 2-3 oz
sliced pancetta (dried bacon)
150 g - 200 g / 3-4 oz
bread crumbs 1 tsp
olive oil 4-5 tbsp
garlic 1-3 cloves
salt, pepper
parsley

Preparation

In a bowl mix the chopped garlic and parsley, a spoonful of olive oil, and salt and pepper.

Lay a slice of ham on each slice of meat (previously beaten if necessary). Then spread a thin layer of the prepared mixture over the ham. Roll up the meat slices. Do it tightly. After that roll up one or two bacon slices around each meat roll, tightly.

Roast the rolls in a grill pan, over medium heat. Soon pour in the wine and and let it almost evaporate. Then add the olive oil, some water, the dalmatian seasoning mix and the bread crumbs.

Continue cooking for 20-30 minutes over moderate heat. From time to time pour in some water and agitate the pot.

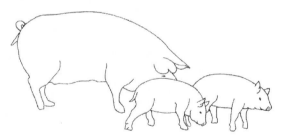

Optional ingredients of the filling: dried bacon, chili pepper, rosemary leaves, vegetable bouillon powder, dalmatian seasoning mix.

Optional herbs and spices for the sauce: rosemary, vegetable bouillon powder or cube, lemon juice and/or zest, garlic, parsley, celery, carrot, onions, basil, bay leaves, raisins, sage, capers, cooking cream, tomato paste, mushrooms, chili pepper, paprika, grated cheese.

Note: Instead of meat rolls, roast the slices of meat and season them while they are still in the pan.

MEAT BALLS

Ingredients

ground pork 250 g / 10 oz
veal 500 g / 1 lb
soft inside of a (thick) bread slice 1
tomato paste 1-3 tsp
garlic 2-3 spicchi
olive oil 7-8 tbsp
bread crumbs
salt, pepper
cloves 2-5
onion 1-2
eggs 1-2
nutmeg
parsley

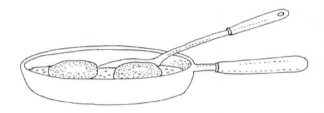

Preparation

In a bowl mix the ground meat, the eggs, the soft inside of a (thick) bread slice (already soaked in milk or water, and then squeezed out), the chopped garlic and parsley, the grated nutmeg, the salt and pepper, and the bread crumbs (adding it with caution). Shape the meat balls and press them in the bread crumbs (or flour).

Then fry the meat balls in some oil, sligtly and quite briefly, over medium heat.

In a pot warm up the oil and fry the chopped onions over low heat. Then add some bread crumbs, not much, and stir a few times, still over low heat. After that, stir in the tomato paste, the crushed cloves and a pin-

eat and love Croatia

ch of grated nutmeg. Lay down and arrange the meat balls (browned on the outside, raw inside). Pour in a cup of water, not covering the balls completely. Cook over moderate heat for 1-1.5 hours.

Optional ingredients of the meat ball mixture: grated cheese, fresh cheese, ricotta cheese, pancetta (dried bacon), mortadella, sausages, mushrooms, green olives, olives stuffed with red bell peppers or chili peppers, raisins soaked in water and squeezed out, pine nuts, grated carrots, vegetable bouillon powder, basil, chives, marjoram, sage, oregano, lemon zest, capers, shallots, butter, wild fennel, flour, sugar, cinammon, mustard, rice flakes, corn flour, milk, cream, grated cauliflower, ground almonds, mint, rosemary, cooked rice, fried onions, egg yolks instead of whole eggs, mozzarella, ham, cooked potatoes.

Optional herbs and spices of the sauce: bread crumbs, pancetta (dried bacon), dry white wine, red wine, beer, dried mushrooms, grated carrots, garlic, basil, parsley, sweet wine, cream, mustard, vegetable bouillon powder, honey, cinnamon, rosemary, capers, mint, leeks, celery, bell peppers, mushrooms, potatoes, peas, lemon zest, sage.

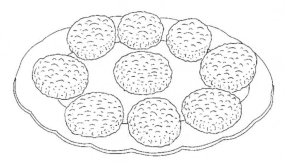

Note: Instead of being braised, the meat balls may be roasted or fried.

CUTLETS WITH ROSEMARY

Ingredients

veal, pork or lamb cutlets 1 kg / 2 lb
olive oil or butter 4-5 tbsp
dry white wine
200-300 ml / 1-1½ cup
(fresh) rosemary
salt

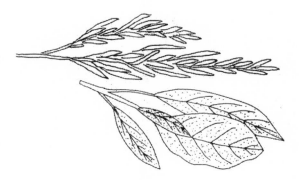

Preparation

Warm up the oil in a pan. Brown briefly the cutlets and then season with chopped rosemary and salt. Pour in the wine and continue cooking for 5-6 minutes.

Optional ingredients: peas or potatoes, cooked but not thoroughly.

PASHTITSADA

Ingredients

veal, beef or sheep
(silverside or a similar cut)
1.25-2kg (3-4.5 lb)
tomatoes 3-4 or tomato paste 1 tbsp
desert wine (prosek) 100-200 ml
bread crumbs 1-2 tbsp
red wine 150-200 ml
vinegar 200-300 ml
bacon 150 g / 5 oz
garlic 7-10 cloves
dry prunes 7-10
olive oil 100 ml
celery root 1
salt, pepper
onions 2-4
cloves 5-6
carrot 1-4
nutmeg

Slow-cooked beef prepared in a rich red sweet and sour sauce, usually served with gnocchi or pasta. Pashtitsada is the best known traditional Dalmatian dish. The oldest known recipe for this beef stew dates back to the 15th century.

Not only that every city has its own

version the method of preparation of this dish, but the recipes vary even from household to household.

Preparation

Cut the bacon in small squares or strips.

Cut the garlic cloves in medium-thin sections across the length of the clove.

Peel the carrots and the celery root and grate them.

Peel the onions and chop them finely.

Peel the tomatoes and cut them to pieces.

Soak the plums in a glass of water.

Pierce the meat with a sharp pointed knife (cut small openings) and insert pieces of garlic, bacon and cloves in it.

Place the meat in a large bowl. Cover with vinegar and some water and leave it overnight in the refrigerator.

The next day, remove the meat from the marinade (keep the latter aside) and dab it with kitchen paper.

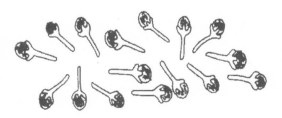

Warm up some olive oil in an appropriate pan. Roast the meat briefly. Remove the meat when it takes on the color from all sides

Fry the onions in the pot, in olive oil, over low heat. Stir in the bread crumbs and then add the carrots and the celery root. Stir a couple of times and put in the tomatoes.

Keep the ingredients cooking for 1-2 minutes and then put in the meat. Pour in the wine and some water.

Cover the pot and continue cooking, over medium heat for 5-10 minutes and then lower the heat and cook over low heat, for the next 2-3 hours. If needed, pour in some water, every now and then. After 1,5 hours add the soaked plums, cut to pieces.

When the meat is tender, take it out and let it cool down, enough to enable slicing it. Then filter the sauce left in the pot.

Thick slices of cooked meat put once more in the pot and cover it with the filtered sauce. Season with grated nutmeg, crushed cloves, and salt and pepper.

Keep on cooking the meat for another half an hour.

DALMATIAN STEAK

Ingredients

pork, chicken or veal meat cutlets
600-700 g / 20-25 oz
vegetable bouillon powder or
dalmatian seasoning mix
1-3 tsp
grated cheese
80-120 g /3-5 oz
bread crumbs
frying oil
eggs 3-5
flour
salt

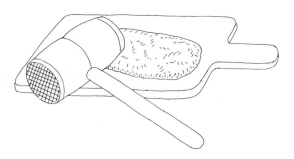

Preparation

Roll the (thin) meat cutlets or smaller slices, also thin, in the grated cheese, pressing firmly, and then in flour, also pressing firmly.

Beat the eggs in a bowl. Stir in the vegetable bouillon powder or dalmatian seasoning mix and some water (not much).

After that, dip the cutlets in beaten eggs.

Then roll the cutlets in the breadcrumbs. Do not press the meat into the breadcrumbs!

Fry the breaded cutlets in an abundent quantity of hot (but not too hot) oil. The oil should be deep, letting the meat to swim in it. Do not crowd the pan.

Take the fried breaded cutlets out of the oil after they turn golden yellow.

Note: Pounding the meat cutlets or slices before coating, makes the meat thinner and also tenderizes it.

VEAL STEW

Ingredients

veal 1.25 kg / 3 lb
pancetta (dried bacon) 60-80 g / 2 oz
ripe tomatoes 400-800 g /1-2 lb
red wine 200 ml / 1 cup
olive oil 4-5 tbsp
garlic 1-2 cloves
salt, pepper
carrots 2-3
celery 1 rib
onions 1

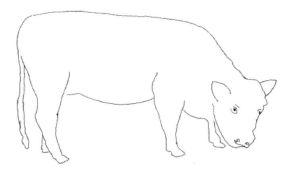

Preparation

Cut one carrot into short sticks and the other into small cubes.

Chop the onion, garlic and celery.

Peel the tomatoes and cut them into pieces.

Cut the pancetta (dried bacon) into short sticks.

Incise narrow holes in the meat and in some of them insert the carrot sticks and into others the pancetta sticks. Then repeatedly tie up the meat with a kitchen string.

Warm up the oil in a pan. Fry the chopped onions, over low heat. Then add the celery, carrot cubes and garlic. Stir a few times and lay down the meat. Raise the heat and brown the meat shortly all around. Then pour in the wine and let it almost evaporate. After that add the tomatoes and season with salt and pepper. Cook for 2-4 hours, over low heat. At the end cut the meat into slices, not too thin. Season the meat slices with the meat sauce.

Optional herbs and spices: basil, garlic, nutmeg, cloves, tomato paste, vegetable bouillon powder.

LAMB STEW

Ingredients

lamb meat 1 kg / 2 lb
dry white wine 100-200 ml / ½ - 1 cup
olive oil 4-5 tbsp
garlic 1-2 cloves
bay leaves 2-3
sale, pepe
rosemary

Preparation

eat and love Croatia

Cut the lamb meat into a 5-6 pieces. Chop the garlic and the rosemary leaves.

Warm up the oil in a pan. Brown lightly the lamb cuts. Then add the the bay leaves, rosemary and garlic. Pour in the wine and let it almost evaporate.

Continue cooking, adding some water every now and then, over medium heat, for approximately half an hour.

Optional ingredients: chili peppers, paprika, onions, carrots, mustard, vegetable bouillon powder.

LAMB IN WINE

Ingredients

lamb 1-1.25 kg / 2-3 lb
dry white wine 200 ml / 1 cup
(white) vinegar 2-5 tbsp
olive oil 4-5 tbsp
garlic 1-2 cloves
potatoes 1 lb
salt, pepper
rosemary
flour
sage

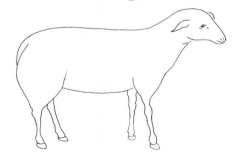

Preparation

Peel the potatoes and cut them into cubes, not to small. Chop the garlic, rosemary and sage.

Cut the lamb meat into 6-7 pieces. Press them in flour.

Warm up the oil in a pot and fry briefly the pieces of meat, over medium heat. Then add the garlic, rosemary and sage.

Pour in the wine and vinegar and let them almost evaporate. Then pour in some water and add the potatoes. Cook over medium heat for 30-40 minutes.

Optional primary ingredients: ham, cut into cubes, chili peppers, desalted anchovy fillets.

Possible omissions: If the potatoes are omitted, there is no need for the baking phase.

SOPARNIK

Ingredients

(swiss) chard 1-1.25 kg
(green) onions 1-3
olive oil 3-5 tbsp
garlic 3-4 cloves
water 250 ml
salt, pepper
flour 500 g
parsley

Soparnik is a pie with a chard filling. It is a specialty of the Dalmatian region of Poljica, ranging from Omiš to Split.

Preparation

Wash the chard and then cut the leaves into strips. Place the chard in a bowl.

Finely chop the onions and parsley and add them to the chard. Season with salt, pepper and some olive oil, not much.

In a bowl sieve the flour and add the salt, some olive oil and water. Then mix everything together. Make the classic dough.

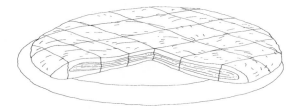

Sprinkle some flour on a baking tray and put half of the thinly rolled dough on it.

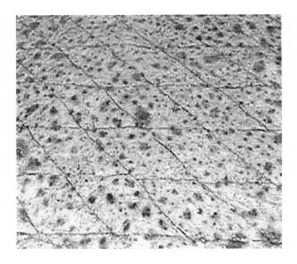

Add the chard, onion and parsley mixture on.

Cover with the other half of the dough, also thinly rolled.

Tuck in and pinch the edges so it is all closed around.

Place in the oven at 200°C for around 20 minutes.

Crush the garlic and add it to some olive oil and apply it to the top of the baked pie.

MEAT PIE

Ingredients

ground veal, beef or pork 750 g

commercially produced fillo dough
500 g
vegetable bouillon powder
1 tsp
olive oil 3-4 tbsp
salt, pepper
onions 2-3
eggs 1-2

Preparation

Warm the olive oil in a pan and put in the chopped onions. Fry over low heat for 4-5 minutes.

Add the ground meat to the onions and cook for another 5-6 minutes over medium heat. Season with vegetable bouillon powder, a pinch of salt (carefully) and some pepper.

eat and love Croatia

After that, remove the meat from the stove and let it cool down for a couple of minutes.

Lay a couple of sheets of fillo dough into the greased baking pan and drizzle with water and oil.

Spread some of the meat filling along the dough sheet and repeat layering, and drizzling with oil and water, until the filling is used up.

Handle the thin dough sheets gently but don't worry if they tear.

Place the pan in the pre-heated oven and bake at 180°C/350°F for 25- 40 minutes, until the top of the pie turns to golden brown.

Once cooked, cover with a baking paper to keep the moisture and cool down for 10 minutes.

Slice the meat pie in squares and serve it warm.

Optional ingredients: braised mushrooms, parsley, sweet paprika, garlic, rosemary, milk, sour cream, cooking cream, beaten eggs, dry bacon, grated cheese, raisins, nutmeg, tomato paste.

Note: The term phyllo (also spelled filo or fillo) dough, which means "leaf" in Greek, stands for thin sheets of dough.

CHEESE PIE

Ingredients

commercially produced fillo dough 500 g
butter or olive oil 5-6 tbsp
sour cream 200-400 ml

fresh cheese 0.75-1 kg
eggs 2-3
salt

Preparation

Mix the cheese, cream, eggs, butter, or oil, and salt in a bowl.

Lay a couple of sheets of fillo dough into the greased baking pan and drizzle with water and oil.

Spread some of the cheese filling along the dough sheet and repeat layering, and drizzling with oil and water, until the filling is used up.

Handle the thin dough sheets gently but don't worry if they tear.

Place the pan in the pre-heated oven and bake at 180°C/350°F for 25- 40 minutes, until the top of the pie turns to golden brown.

Once cooked, cover with a baking paper to keep the moisture and cool down for 10 minutes. After that slice the cheese pie in squares and serve.

Optional ingredients: gorgonzola, grated cheese, feta cheese, ham.

Note: Butchnitza, the squash and cottage cheese pie, is very similar to the standard cheese pie.

RABBIT STEW

Ingredients

(wild or domestic) rabbit meat
1.5 kg
dry white wine 100-300 ml
vinegar 300-400 ml
olive oil 4-5 tbsp
garlic 2-3 cloves
salt, pepper
onions 2-3
bay leaves
rosemary
lemon 1
parsley

Marinade

Arrange the pieces of rabbit meat in a bowl and pour over the vinegar and also some water. Let it soak through the night. In the morning, pour out the liquid and let the rabbit meat drain off for an hour or two.

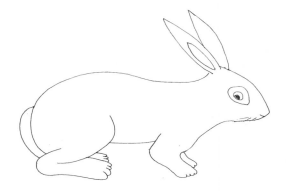

Optional ingredients of the marinade: bay leaves, rosemary, onions, carrots, celery root, garlic, celery leaves, parsley, sage, cloves, pepper, vegetable bouillon powder, wine.

Preparation

Chop and mince the onions, garlic, parsley and rosemary. Grate the lemon zest and then squize the juice. Warm the oil in a pot and put the chopped onions in. Fry for 4-5 minutes over low heat. Then add the garlic and parsley. Stir a couple of times and put in the meat. Stir again and add the rosemary, lemon juice and lemon zest.

eat and love Croatia

Continue the cooking rabbit meat over medium heat for 15 minutes and then pour in the wine and after a couple of minutes lower the heat.

Optional ingredients: bread crumbs, cooking cream, vegetable bouillon powder, sugar, meat soup cube, desert wine, tomato paste, paprika, nutmeg, cloves, olives, capers, sage.

PEKA

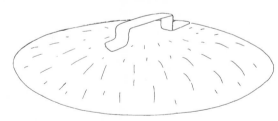

Peka (baking under the bell) is a famous Dalmatian dish. Ingredients (veal, possibly also lamb meat, potatoes, onions, oil and other seasonings) are placed in a pan and subsequently covered with a bell-shaped lid and ambers, and after that follows the roasting.

Optional ingredients: carrots, garlic, bell peppers, white cabbage, eggplants, wine, sausages.

LAMB WITH PEAS

Ingredients

lamb meat 1-1.2 kg
peas (fresh or frozen) 500 g
sweet paprika 0.5 tsp
olive oil 4-5 tbsp
tomatoes 2-3
bell pepper 1
celery root 1
salt, pepper
carrots 1-2
onions 1-2
cloves 1-2
cinnamon
parsley

Preparation

Cut the lamb meat into large pieces.

Chop the onions and parsley. Grate the carrots and the celery root. Cut the bell pepper in pieces. Peel the tomatoes and dice them.

Warm the oil in a pot. Put in the onions, let them fry for a couple of minutes, and then add the bell pepper, carrots, celery and tomatoes. Cook for another 3-4 minutes over medium heat and then put in the meat.

Continue cooking over medium heat. Stir occasionally. Pour in some water when necessary.

Add the peas to the meat, not being already completelly softened.

Season with the sweet paprika, parsley, cinnamon, cloves, salt and pepper.

Cook over low heat until the peas soften enough.

Optional ingredients: potatoes, broad beans, dried bacon, red or dry white wine, vegetable bouillon powder, rosemary, peperoncino, nutmeg, raisins, garlic, dry figs, bay leaves, cooking cream, bread crumbs.

BRAISED TRIPE

Ingredients

pre-boiled beef honecomb tripe
(cut into short strips)
or
lamb tripe, in strips,
1 kg / 2 lbs
fresh or canned tomatoes 2-5,
tomato passata 100-500 ml,
or
homemade tomato sauce
150-300 ml
olive oil 4-5 tbsp
garlic 1-2 cloves
salt, pepper
onions 1-2

Preparation

Peel and finely chop the onions and garlic.

Warm the oil in a pot. Put in the onions, let them fry for a few minutes, and then add the garlic.

Stir a couple of times and put in the tripe, already partially precooked.

Continue cooking over medium heat. Stir occasionally. Pour in some water when necessary.

Serve the tripe sprinkled with finely grated hard cheese or vinegar or both.

Optional ingredients: dry white wine, dried bacon, carrots, potatoes, peas, vegetable bouillon powder or cube, mint, vinegar, rosemary, celery, dalmatian seasoning mix, grated cheese, cheese crest, ham, boiled beans, green olives, peperoncino, bread crumbs, beef meat sauce, basil, lemon zest, lemon thyme, sage, small white beans, precooked, red or yellow bell peppers.

Another method

The simplest way to prepare the tripe is to boil it in water.

Drain off the cooked tripe and season it with olive oil, vegetable bouillon powder, salt, pepper.

Note: Tripe sauce is excellent with pasta. For that purpose, the tripe may be crushed in the sauce, before seasoning the pasta.

Warm the oil in a pot. Put in the onions, let them fry for a couple of minutes, over low heat and then add the potatoes and tomatoes, and also the rosemary and bay leaves.

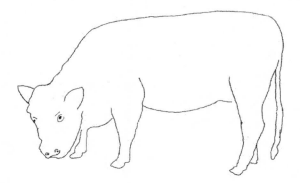

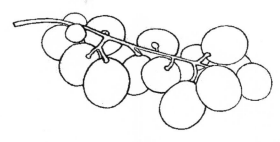

Suggestion: The liquid, the tripe sauce contains, may be reduced more or less. Depending on that, a fork or a spoon may be used to eat the dish.

Cook for another 2-3 minutes over medium heat, stirring all the time, and then put in the meat and the grape berries.

MEAT WITH GRAPES AND POTATOES

Ingredients

veal, pork or lamb meat 1 kg
mature white grapes 150-200 g
fresh or canned tomatoes 2-5,
tomato passata 100-500 ml,
or
tomato paste 1-2 tbsp
potatoes 500-750 g
olive oil 4-5 tbsp
salt, pepper
bay leaves
rosemary

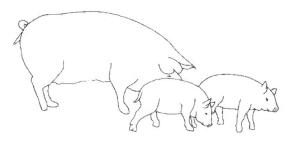

Continue cooking over medium heat. Stir occasionally. Pour in some water when necessary.

Preparation

Cut the meat into large pieces. Chop the onions and rosemary. Peel the tomatoes and potatoes and dice them coarsely. Cut every grape berry in half, removing the seeds.

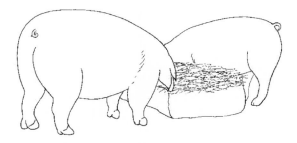

Optional ingredients: fresh-squeezed grape juice, mushrooms, peas, leeks, broad beans, carrots, thyme, garlic, vegetable bouillon powder, dalmatian seasoning mix.

MEAT SLICES IN A SIMPLE SAUCE

Ingredients

thin pork or veal slices 1 kg
olive oil 4-5 tbsp
flour 3-4 tbsp
salt, pepper

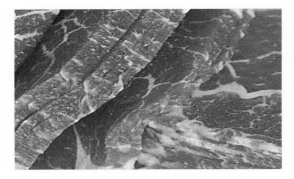

Preparation

Roll the meat slices in flour.

Warm up the oil in a large pan. Fry the meat slices very briefly over medium heat.

Transfer each batch of the fried meat into a suitable pot. After that transfer also the remaining oil.

Pour in some water, not much. Season with salt and pepper. Keep cooking over low heat as long as it takes for the meat to soften enough. From time to time, pour in some water, not much, and shake the pot.

Optional ingredients: dalmatian seasoning mix, lemon zest, thyme, lemon thyme, vegetable bouillon powder, capers, green pepper grains, tomato passata or paste, cloves, basil, garlic, onions, oregano, rosemary, sage, dry white wine, bay leaves, sweet paprika, celery, mushrooms, cooking cream, peperoncino, green onions, grated carrots, marjoram, fresh squeezed grape juice, gorgonzola, grated cheese.

SARMA

Ingredients

sauerkraut (sour cabbage) 1 head
sauerkraut leaves, cut in strips
500-700 g
vegetable bouillon powder 1 tsp
beef or sheep meat
750-850 g
pork, veal or lamb meat
350-500 g
dried bacon (pancetta)
150-300 g
sweet paprika 1 tsp
onions 1-2
raw rice 150-200 g
olive oil 4-5 tbsp
garlic 3-5 cloves
bread crumbs
salt, pepper
cloves 3-4
eggs 1-2
lemon 1
nutmeg
parsley

Fermented foods have a long history in many cultures, with sauerkraut dishes being amongst the most well-known.

Fermented foods, such as the sauerkraut, were very valuable in the age before refrigeration. The origin of sauerkraut in fact is in China.

Sauerkraut is the finely cut raw cabbage, or the whole cabbage, fermented by the influence of lactic acid. The lactic acid develops as the result of fermenting the sugars in the cabbage leaves, which occurs because of the activity of lactic acid bacteria.

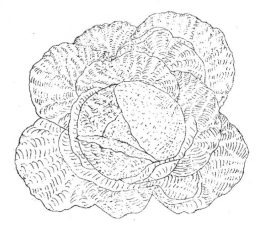

Today sarma, stuffed sauerkraut rolls, is a widely spread dish Croatia, very similar to "arambashichi", a popular Dalmatian specialty from Sinj.

This popular winter meal is widely known all over the Balkan region and the question of its origin is still not resolved as many countries claim it as their own.

Preparation

Spread the filling, prepared with all the ingredients quoted in the recipe, on the sauerkraut leaves, which we-

re already soaked in water during the last night. Roll up the leaves, shaping stuffed rolls.

Lay the stuffed rolls in a large pot, already paved with olive oil, dry bacon pieces and sauerkraut strips, also previously soaked in water.

Pour over the solution of tomato paste in wate

Cover the pot and cook over medium heat, even low, for 3-5 hours, depending on the quantity involved.

MEAT AND POTATO STEW

Ingredients

veal or beef 700-800 g
red or dry white wine 100-300 ml
fresh tomatoes 200-500 g
or
tomato paste 1-3 tbsp
potatoes 500-700 g
garlic 1-3 cloves
olive oil 4-5 tbsp
bay leaves 1-3
salt, pepper
onions 2-4
parsley
flour

Preparation

Cut the meat in pieces. Roll them slightly in flour. Peel the potatoes and cut them in pieces, not too small.

Chop the onions, garlic and parsley. Peel the tomatoes and mince them.

Fry the meat in olive oil and then remove it from the pot. Continue by fry gently the onions and later on add the garlic. Put the meat back and pour in the wine. Keep on cooking over medium heat until the wine almost evaporates.

After that, add the tomatoes and a cou-ple of bay leaves. Season with salt and pepper and cover the pot. Continue cooking until the meat softens enough. Every now and then stir lightly and pour in some water if needed. Add the potatoes and keep on cooking until the potatoes soften. Stir in some finely chopped parsley and remove the pot from the stove.

Optional ingredients: dried bacon, bell peppers, broad beans, peas, paprika powder, green beans, green onions, grapes, carrots, cloves, celery, capers, cinnamon, olives, rosemary, sage, vegetable bouillon powder, lemon zest and/or juice, vinegar, grated cheese, cooking cream, sour cream, chili pepper.

ZELENA MENESTRA

The zelena (green) menestra is a symbolic (winter) dish in the Dubrovnik region, with ancient roots.

In pot with hot water, cook various kinds of (previously soaked) dry meat (pork, sheep), bacon, ribs and other parts, sausages too (but added near the end), until it begins to detach from the bones.

After that, let the boiled meat cool down for a few minutes and then extract the meat from the bones.

Separately, or with the boiled meat, or the boiled meat is added near the end of the cooking process, cook a mixture of vegetables (rashtika, collard greens, kale, savoy cabbage, white cabbage). Peeled potatoes can be added. Cook over medium heat.

A half an hour before the cooking is done, a special seasoning mixture can be added. This may contain lard, olive oil, vegetabel bouillon powder, pepper, salt.

Let the cooked dish rest 15-20 minutes before serving.

Serve the well boiled vegetables, with salt and olive oil, along with the cooked dry meat, suitable cut to slices.

eat and love Croatia

BOSHCARIN

Boshkarin is a delicacy of the Istrian region of Croatia.

Boškarin is actually the name of a native long-horned ox that grazes on Istrian pastures,

The meat of boshkarin oxen is a delicacy served as steaks or fillets, often with Istrian handmade pasta called foozi, seasoned with truffles.

FRITAYA

Istrian omelette made with eggs and other ingredients, such as truffles, asparagus, prosciutto, pancetta, cheese, sausages or mushrooms.

KOTLOVINA

Kotlovina is a meat stew, prepared outdoors, popular in northwest Croatia regions or in Zagreb. It is cooked in a specially designed cauldron over an open fire.

Kotlovina consists of chopped (marinated) pork meat (often also including sausages, chops and ribs),

which is firstly fried, then it is being accompanied with vegetables (onions, peppers, tomatoes, potatoes ...), vegetable bouillon powder, paprika and garlic, possibly white wine also, and after that it is slowly cooked until ready.

LAMB ON THE SPIT

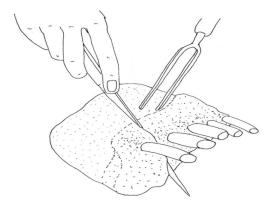

Lamb on the spit has been a favourite method of cooking in Croatia for thousands of years. The quality of the lamb meat and the experience of the cooks make this meal soo good.

CHEVAPI

These grilled skinless sausages, small and finger-shaped, are famous in the whole region. They are usually made of minced beef meat, possibly combined with pork or lamb meat, seasoned with appropriate spices.

After being grilled, the "chevapi", also called "chevapchichi", are stuffed into a round flat bread loaf, with selected supplements - mayonnaise, various sauces, pickled gherkins, onions, cheese, sour cream or other.

eat and love Croatia

ZAGREBATCHKI ODREZAK

Ingredients

veal, pork or chicken meat slices 4-8
cheese slices 100-120 g
ham slices 100-120 g
breadcrumbs
salt, pepper
flour
eggs

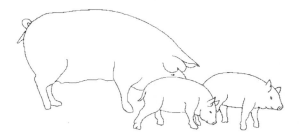

Preparation

Pound the (large) meat slices and season them with salt and pepper. Cover each slice with ham and cheese. Fold one half of each stuffed meat slice over the other half.

Beat the eggs in a bowl. After that, dip the stuffed meat slices in beaten eggs. Then roll the slices in breadcrumbs. Do not press the meat into the breadcrumbs!

Fry the breaded meat in an abundent quantity of hot (but not too hot) oil. The oil should be deep, letting the meat to swim in it. Do not crowd the pan.

Take the fried breaded meat out of the oil after they turn golden yellow.

Note: This cordon bleu type of breaded meat slices are very popular in the Croatia capital Zagreb.

WINE GOULASH

Ingredients

veal meat 500 g
canned whole peeled tomatoes 500-800 g
red or dry white wine 150-200 ml
potatoes 250-400 g
(olive) oil 4-5 tbsp
paprika powder
bay leaves 1-3
cumin seeds
onions 2-4
parsley
salt

Preparation

Dice the meat. Cut the tomatoes to pieces. Peel and then chop the onions. Peel and dice the potatoes. Mince the parsley.

Warm up the oil in a pot. Fry gently the onions. Add the meat dices and the bay leaves. Keep on cooking over medium heat. After half an hour put in the diced potatoes and the rest of the spices.

PORK TENDERLOIN "STUBITZA"

Ingredients

pork tenderloins 4
dry white wine 150-200 ml
cooking cream 100-150 ml

sour cream 200-300 ml
plum brandy 30-40 ml
dry plums 12-20
butter 4-5 tbsp
salt, pepper
parsley

Preparation

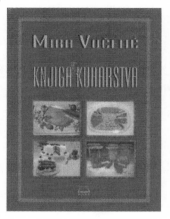

Fill in the tenderloins, previously lenghtwise cut in two, , and not qui- te entirely of course, with dry plums (possibly previously moderately soaked) and also some butter.

Warm up the oil in a pot. Lay down the stuffed tenderloins. Cover them with some chopped dry plums and season with salt and pepper. Pour in the wine.

Continue cooking for 10-15 minutes over medium heat, closer to moderate, and then add the sour and the cooking cream. Keep on cooking over moderate heat for a couple of minutes. At the very end pour in the plum brandy and continue for a minute.

From time to time, during the cook- ing process, shake the pot. Avoid stirring. If necessary, add some wa- ter or, even better, filtered vege- table soup.

Note: This an ancient dish, traditio- nally prepared in the nothern parts of Croatia.

VISOVATZ BEGOVITZA (THE FRANCISCAN BEGOVITZA)

Although the original, centuries old, recipe is guarded in the Franciscan Monastery of of Visovac, this dish can be found in the Skradin resta- urant menues.

The ingredients are marinated lamb meat, local seasoning herbs, sour sheep milk, selected types of potatoes, olive oil, lard, grated cheese.

The other ingredients are still not fully disclosed.

ROASTED TURKEY WITH HOMEMADE MLINTZI

Mlintzi in fa- ct is a thin, dry flatbread that is bro- ken into pie- ces before being cooked in boiling wa- ter. It is then served soak- ing up the ju- ices of a roa- sted turkey, which it is served with.

BARON TRENK STEAK

This dish, actually the meat rolls, popular in the Croatian region of Slavonia, is prepared stuffing the meat slices with the local sauce called "ajvar", thinly sliced famous slavonian sausage "kulen", made of minced pork, paprika, garlic and salt, and boiled eggs, and eventually folding them into rolls.

The rolls are then cooked in oil and wine, possibly even with (sour) cooking cream or mushrooms also.

MEAT FROM TIBLITZA ("MESO Z TIBLICE")

Pork - flavored, smoked and stored, both the meat and the bacon, in a wooden barrel.

TCHOBANATZ

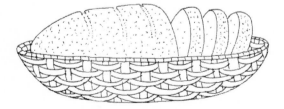

This meat stew is prepared with various types of meat (beef, pork, lamb or game), lots of onions and other vegetables, seasoned with sweet and/or hot paprika.

The stew, often cooked in the open air, must be cooked for hours, over moderate heat.

ZAGORSKI SHTRUKLI

Zagorski shtrukli is a traditional and very popular dish in the Hrvatsko Zagorje and Zagreb regions in the north of Croatia.

Made with cottage cheese, sour cream and eggs, shtrukli can be salty or sweet.

Shtrukli can be either boiled or baked.

ZLIJEVKA

Traditional pastry popular in northern Croatia, made with cottage cheese, eggs and corn flour (sometimes sprinkled with sugar).

eat and love Croatia

SWEETS

ROZATA

Ingredients

milk 500-600 ml
eggs 6-7
sugar, for the custard 7-8 tbsp
sugar, for the caramel 7-8 tbsp
vanilla sugar 2 tbsp
rose liqueur or maraschino or rum
2 tbsp
lemon (grated zest) 1

Rozata is a dessert that is spread in the entire Dalmatia, but it is particularly popular in Dubrovnik. Similar to French creme caramel, it's an egg cream topped with delicious caramel, modified by the addition of sweet liqueur made from rose petals (hence comes its name).

Preparation

With a mixer, beat the eggs and the sugar until it is creamy. Add the milk, lemon zest, maraschino and vanilla, and mix well.

Place the sugar in a saucepan and cook over low and medium heat un-

til the sugar syrup caramelise and turns golden brown.

Pour the caramel into the bottom of the moulds. Let the caramel cool.

Pour the milk, sugar and egg mixture into the moulds. Cook the rozata in a bain-marie - a large pot filled with enough hot water to come halfway up the sides of the moulds — for about 40 minutes.

Remove the rozata from the oven or from the stove and transfer it to the refrigerator for a few hours.

Remove the rozata from the refrigerator and turn the rozata out onto a plate, letting the caramel liquid from the bottom of the mould fill the plate around the dessert.

HONEY COOKIES

Ingredients

flour 1 kg
honey 300-500 g
grated lemon zest
baking soda 1 tsp
crushed cloves
egg yolks 3-4
milk 2-3 tbsp
butter 300 g
cinnamon

In an suitable pot warm up the honey. Pour it into a bowl and mix it with all the other ingredients, making a dough. Format the dough into round shapes, not too thin, not too small.

Bake the cookies briefly, over medium heat, and then take them from the oven. Let them cool down a bit, and serve them.

Optional ingredients: (brown) sugar, ground almonds, ground hazelnuts, grated chocolate, orange zest, lemon juice, grated nutmeg, salt, lard.

ARANTZINI

Arantzini (Arancini) are made of (organic) orange zest, cut to strips, cooked with sugar, and then left to dry out.

Before drying, arantzini can be dipped in melted chocolate,

MANTALA

Ingredients

ripe red grapes 12-15 kg
semolina (grits) 1-2 kg
grated nutmeg 1-2 tsp
ground cloves 1-2 tsp
almonds 500-750 g
cinnamon 1-2 tsp

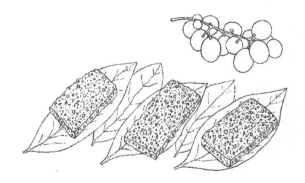

This cake, made of concentrated grape must, in the region is also called kumpet, kunfet, chookter or choopter.

Preparation

Cook the grape must (traditionally of the local grape sorts "kadarun" and "dalmatinka") over medium to low heat for 5-10 hours, until it thickens and reduces its volume to a third or even to a fourth of its original volume.

When the must reaches its desired thickness, stir in the semolina (grits), as much as the thickened must will take. After that, cook for another half an hour, stirring all the time.

When the mantala paste thickens so much that it becomes hard to stir,

126

put in the almonds, cloves, nutmeg and cinnamon.

In a wooden box with low sides, lay a white cloth, sprinkle it sparingly with cinnamon and then pour in the mantala paste. Level the surface and sprinkle it with cinnamon.

Let the mantala rest for a few days in a dry and cool place. After that cut it and serve.

Optional ingredients: minced walnuts, lemon or orange zest, orange juice, grated lemons or quinces, coriander or vanilla sugar.

Note: (White) mantala is prepared with white grape must.

Note: Mantala can be prepared also using the fruits of the strawberry tree (locally called "maginje").

STONSKI MACARULI

Ingredients

for the filling

pasta (penne, rigatoni or ziti) 300-400 g
grated dark chocolate 50-100 g
ground almonds 120-150 g
ground walnuts 150-200 g
icing sugar 30-50 g
butter 200-250 g
sugar 200-250 g
cinnamon 1 tsp
rum 2 tbsp
eggs 4-6
lemon 1

for the pastry

flour 350-400 g
vinegar 1 tsp
olive oil tbsp
eggs 1
water
salt

The Ston macaruli, also called the Ston cake, is a regional specialty that combines pasta with chocolate and a pinch of cinnamon.

Preparation

Mix the ingredients of the pastry in a suitable bowl. After kneading the dough, cover it with a cloth and let it rest until the filling is ready.

Lightly beat the eggs in a glass, with the icing sugar, and save them for further use.

In another bowl mix all the other ingredients of the filling.

In the meanwhile cook the pasta, minding not to overcook it, and drain it well.

Preheat the oven to app. 180°. Oil the bacing pan and dust it with flour.

Roll the pastry into a circle more than big enough to fit into the base of the prepared baking pan and overhang down the sides of it.

Carefully lift the rolled pastry into the pan. Spread the filling into the base of the pastry in the pan. Top with several slices of butter. Place a single layer of cooked pasta over the top, then sprinkle over more of the filling mixture. Dot with slices of butter.

Repeat this process with the remaining pasta, filling mixture and butter.

When you reach the top, evenly pour the beaten eggs over the filling. Gather the overhanging pastry over the filling. Press the pastry down and put a few more of the butter slices. Place the pan into the oven and bake for about 1 hour, until the surface becomes golden. Allow to cool before taking the pan out.

FIGS IN HONEY

Ingredients

figs 8-12
ground almonds 150 g
honey 5-8 tbsp
butter 150 g
rum

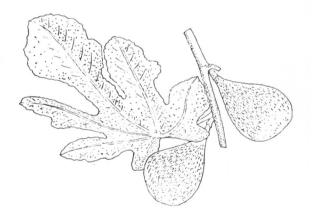

Preparation

Stir a small quantity of rum into the honey. In a pan warm up the butter and put in the figs, each cut in two halves. Fry them lightly. Pour the honey over the figs, not all at once. Keep warming over low heat, not long. Then remove the pan with the figs from the heat and sprinkle the ground almonds over the figs.

SAMOBORSKE CREMSHNITE

A tasty square cake layered with vanilla, cream and whipped cream.

This cake is a "must eat" when in the town of Samobor.

Samoborska kremšnita features two layers of puff pastry, which are in between filled mainly with a cream layer. On top of this cream is a layer of whipped cream, rather thin.

The top layer of puff pastry is sprinkled with powdered sugar.

SOUR CHERRY STRUDEL

A wide range of strudels, especially the sour cherry (maraska, characteristic for the region of Zadar, is the best known variety) strudel, is a traditional dessert Croatia is widely known for.

POVITITZA

This filled bread, an Istrian (but not exclusively) specialty, is made with a yeast-raised dough that is stretched out or rolled thinly and then spread

on with a filling usually of walnuts, butter, cocoa, vanilla, sugar, egg yolk and milk.

VARAZDINSKI KLIPITCHI

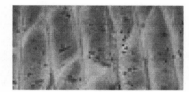

This delicious pastry iz popular in the city of Varazdin region.

RAPSKA TORTA

Cakes are popular in Croatia. Some are even a real delicacy. Such is the Rapska torta, a traditional cake prepared on the island of Rab.

MAKARSKA TORTA

This cake, the Makarana cake, is famous because of its originality and exquisite taste.

GIBANITZA

This layered cake prepared with poppy seeds, apples, walnuts and cottage cheese is popular in the region of Medjimurje.

A FEW MORE
WORDS

The first and the utmost important step, even before the beginning of the cooking process, is to purchase only the first quality ingredients, as fresh as possible.

The secret why some dishes taste better than others lies not only in the balance of the components used, but also in the sequence and the timing when they are to be added during the process of cooking a dish.

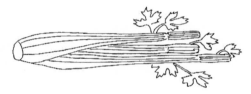

Do not put too many different herbs and spices into the food you are preparing.

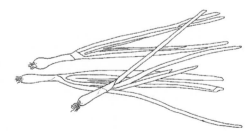

Add the seasonings gradually, tasting the food more than once in order to balance the flavours.

Do not rush and do not overheat in order to speed up the cooking process. The slow cooking of food deeply enhances its flavour.

Your creativity in the process of preparing food is always welcome. But, at the same time, do not forget to honor the fact that the basic recipe usually reflects the centuries lasting effort of our predecessors to find the perfect taste of the dish.

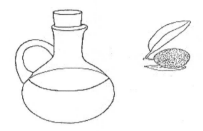

A chosen sauce for pasta or rice sometimes may be prepared not only by warming up the ingredients during the process but also by mixing and blending without heating.

Never cover the pan in which you cook a sauce.

The preparation of a meal does not start on the stove, but with the selection of fresh and appropriate food.

Quotes and aphorisms

''Some people ask the secret of our long marriage. We take time to go to a restaurant two times a week. A little candlelight, dinner, soft music and dancing. She goes Tuesdays, I go Fridays.'' Henny Youngman

"Forgive me, love! No! No! It is not true that you are not a good cook. Lately the cold buttered spaghetti were always cold to the right point! "
Rocco Barbaro

''When the waitress asked if I wanted my pizza cut into four or eight slices, I said ''Four. I don't think I can eat eight.'' Yogi Berra

I said "Where do you want to go for your anniversary?" She said: "I want to go somewhere I've never been before." I said "Try the kitchen."
Henny Youngman

'' The cake must always be remarkable because it comes after you're no longer hungry. ''Alexandre Grimod

''The man also eats with his eyes, especially if the waitress is pretty.''
Ugo Tognazzi

"A recipe is a story that always ends with a good meal. But when I cook, the end becomes uncertain.'' Pat Conroy

"I always cook with wine, sometimes I even add it to the food." W.C. Fields

"Italians have only two things on their mind. The other one is spaghetti."
Catherine Deneuve

''The trouble with eating Italian food is that three or four days later you're hungry again.'' George Miller

''I have removed all the bad food from the house. It was delicious.''

INDEX

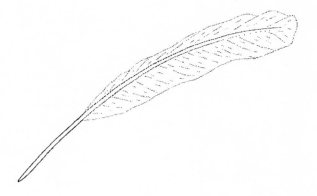

Made in the USA
Middletown, DE
25 September 2021